Knowing the Children We Teach

Knowing the Children We Teach

Essays on Music Learning

Danette Littleton and Meryl Sole

Published in cooperation with the
National Association for Music Education

ROWMAN & LITTLEFIELD
Lanham • Boulder • New York • London

Published in cooperation with the National Association for Music Education, 1806 Robert Fulton Drive, Reston, Virginia 20191; nafme.org

Published by Rowman & Littlefield
An imprint of The Rowman & Littlefield Publishing Group, Inc.
4501 Forbes Boulevard, Suite 200, Lanham, Maryland 20706
www.rowman.com

86-90 Paul Street, London EC2A 4NE

Copyright © 2023 by Danette Littleton and Meryl Sole

All rights reserved. No part of this book may be reproduced in any form or by any electronic or mechanical means, including information storage and retrieval systems, without written permission from the publisher, except by a reviewer who may quote passages in a review.

British Library Cataloguing in Publication Information Available

Library of Congress Cataloging-in-Publication Data

Names: Littleton, Danette, 1942- author. | Sole, Meryl, 1978- author.
Title: Knowing the children we teach : essays on music learning / Danette Littleton and Meryl Sole.
Description: Lanham, Maryland : Rowman & Littlefield, 2023. | "Published in cooperation with the National Association for Music Education." | Includes bibliographical references and index.
Identifiers: LCCN 2022054898 (print) | LCCN 2022054899 (ebook) | ISBN 9781475866001 (cloth) | ISBN 9781475866018 (paperback) | ISBN 9781475866025 (ebook)
Subjects: LCSH: Music—Instruction and study. | Child development. | Child psychology.
Classification: LCC MT1 .L688 2023 (print) | LCC MT1 (ebook) | DDC 780.71—dc23/eng/20230105
LC record available at https://lccn.loc.gov/2022054898
LC ebook record available at https://lccn.loc.gov/2022054899

♾️ The paper used in this publication meets the minimum requirements of American National Standard for Information Sciences—Permanence of Paper for Printed Library Materials, ANSI/NISO Z39.48-1992.

To all the children who informed our teaching
by their wisdom and goodness

To all the teachers who generously shared their stories

To our families, for their support and love

Contents

Prelude		ix
Part I: Perspectives		**1**
Essay 1	Born to Be Good	3
Essay 2	Music and the Aesthetics of Care	11
Essay 3	What Children Need	23
Essay 4	Music and the Spiritual Child	33
Part II: Pedagogy		**45**
Essay 5	Children's Play with Music	47
Essay 6	Wonder-Filled Knowing and Learning	59
Part III: Promises		**65**
Essay 7	Knowing Those Who Teach	67
Essay 8	Toward a Pedagogy of Hope	77
	Postlude: Compassion, Empathy, and Kindness	85

Appendix	89
Works Cited	113
Index	121
About the Authors	129

Prelude

For America's children, these are not the best of times. Despite our power and riches, millions of children are homeless, underfed, living in poverty, and attending crumbling and moldy schools. The poorest of the poor are under age five, and 71 percent of these are children of color (Dawson 2021). Inequality in education for children in poor neighborhoods continues to deprive them of opportunities afforded those better situated. Since 1954, laws and efforts of goodwill to integrate schools have eroded. Once again, in many cities and towns, Black children attend underserved, underfunded, segregated schools.

In 1860, the Bureau of Indian Affairs established the first of many Indian boarding schools. Thousands of children were removed from their families to be "assimilated" to the "American way of life." It was not until the passage of the Indian Child Welfare Act of 1978 that Indian families gained the legal right to keep their children from being removed to boarding schools (Northern Plains Reservation Aid 2011).

From the early twentieth century, child factory workers led appalling lives of servitude. When there were too many mouths to feed and too little income, tenement children were sent away as farmhands and domestics. For generations, working children were unable to attend school and thus were destined to perpetual poverty.

> The golf links lie so near the mill
> That almost every day
> The laboring children look out
> And see the men at play.
>
> —Sarah N. Cleghorn (quoted in Schuman 2017)

In 1938, Franklin Delano Roosevelt signed into law the Fair Labor Standards Act. It protected children from long hours and dangerous working conditions and set the legal working age to sixteen.

However, today, some of the children we teach are migrant workers, others are children of illegal immigrants who are exploited for their labor, and many are homeless. We have yet to fully understand the impact the COVID-19 pandemic and lockdown has had on our children. Research indicates that the pandemic's greatest negative impact will be suffered by children in poor socioeconomic groups. Many of these children did not have access to enough food, health care, community support, or high-speed internet service when only remote instruction was available. Their world came to a grinding halt in the spring of 2020. Together with educational deficits, the pandemic brought severe medical and mental health complications for children, including increased symptoms of anxiety, depression, irritability, boredom, inattention, loneliness, and fear. We will only begin to understand the suffering of our children and the long-term negative effects of this global crisis as time allows. Moreover, the tragedies of gun violence, its devastation and heartbreak, cause parents and children to live in fear of the next school massacre.

Many children we teach are blessed with advantages of comfort, safety, and enrichment. It is vitally important that we *know* each child we teach, that we understand who they are and what their life is like. It is on this foundation that we develop our best instructional plans and environments, nurture children's musicality, inspire their creativity, and promote lives of well-being and love of learning.

Thus, the fundamental question that guides this inquiry is, Who are the children we teach? While this approach to music education is atypical, it is nonetheless important that we better understand children to enhance their music learning and improve our teaching. As music educators, we are generally well prepared on *what* to teach, somewhat less well prepared about *how* to teach, and even less prepared with knowledge and understanding of *who* we teach. In this book, we submit that what we know about children exerts a powerful influence on their trust and engagement with us and their willingness to participate in learning music. Each child is uniquely sensitive to what we say and as well as to the nonverbal expressions that convey what we think about them. *If a child smiles at you, smile back so they know the world is a good place.*

Investigations from cultural anthropology and sociology (Mead 1951; Keltner 2009; Bregman 2019), concerning the lives of children in the past and in the present, inform and guide our understanding of the children in our music classrooms. In the present work, we seek to bring attention to the constituent parts of learning and teaching from the child's perspective. We want to know what music means to children. Are there interconnections between children's psychological needs and their emotional responses to music, such as joy and delight, comfort and care, curiosity and imagination? How might our classroom environments and pedagogies reach children of *all* cultural identities and social distinctions, especially those who are hurt, angry, withdrawn, or disruptive? Essential to the questions posed here are teachers' thoughts and beliefs about learners' behaviors and emotional states.

Unexamined, but no less important, is the interdependent relationship between learner and teacher, child and adult, regarding attributes of empathy and respect. The present work examines perspectives and pedagogies of music learning and teaching and suggests that music is uniquely positioned to provide opportune conditions of trust and care. Through music, we can help each child learn to regulate emotion, overcome behavioral difficulties, and experience personal joy in creating and making music. Children's experiences of music, like our own, are attuned to distinct affinities and exactitudes of meaning. *What music means is how it feels.*

Knowing the Children We Teach is organized into three parts: Perspectives, Pedagogy, and Promises, with subsequent chapters as stand-alone essays conceptually connected, yet distinctive, and supported by relevant research data. Included are video ethnographies and interviews from teachers, performers, songwriters, and professors in music education and social work.

Methodology

Prior to the present study, for two years Dr. Sole conducted a pilot study with graduate students enrolled in music education courses. They revealed rich and detailed responses about teaching and learning when one idea seemed to trigger the next in their narratives. With reference to Vivian Paley (1999), they began to consider themselves as "anecdotalists" telling "little stories."

Our method of data collection was derived, in part, from Fox and Cayari (2016), Cayari and Fox (2013), and Ong, Swanto, and Alsaqqaf (2020), who used video to collect teachers' personal reflections on their teaching practices. Presented here is a qualitative case study conducted for fourteen months with thirty-five music teachers. Participants came from all regions of the United States—rural, urban, and suburban. Combined, they represent music educators at all stages of their careers, from new teachers to seasoned and retired educators, and from diverse backgrounds, ethnicities, training, and experiences. Each teacher was asked to respond to a series of prompts by means of video ethnographies, or video reflection journals. Participants were invited to reflect on all or some of the following:

- Have you had children who exhibited specific behaviors in the classroom: disruptive, joyous, angry, comedic?
- Can you reflect on a specific child and your experience with that child?
- What are some of your most unforgettable experiences with children?
- What did you learn in school about teaching children that you have found to be invaluable?
- What did you not learn in school that you learned through teaching children?
- What do you wish you had studied or learned about children in school before you began teaching?
- What experiences or practices have you discovered in your position as a music teacher that you could share with other teachers?
- As a young child, what were you like in school—timid and shy, unsettled, unruly, confident and assertive?
- Did you feel welcomed and included as a child at school?
- What music activities were your favorites?
- What do you remember about your music teacher?

Data Analysis[1]

Each teacher's reflections were transcribed verbatim and systematically coded according to the themes that emerged through analysis: the nature and traits of children; kindness and care; musicality; musical play and spontaneous musical behaviors; spirituality; acquisition of skill, knowledge, and understanding; promises to keep; and insights on teacher training. Most participants submitted video recordings of themselves responding to the prompts, while a few chose to submit audio recordings or written responses. The video ethnographies ranged in length from five to sixty-five minutes. After initial analysis, we continued to revisit the data to see if additional themes emerged. Indeed, we found new and related data as we reread the transcripts, such as additional key words and significant themes and patterns. In some cases, we conducted follow-up sessions with participants for comments they might have on new themes. We found that a few teachers referred to their own experiences as parents and explained how parenting impacted their understanding of children and their teaching.

General Observations

Music teachers reported that they designed lessons to be responsive to children's needs—the need for relationships, safety, individuality, developmentally appropriate experiences, structure, and supportive communities (Brazelton and Greenspan 2000). When teacher-participants observed that children's needs were not being met, they altered their teaching and individualized their approach, often putting the children's needs ahead of musical goals. They referenced the innate kindness of children and responded with acts of loving care in recognition of the intrinsic goodness of children and humankind. Teachers practiced yoga and meditation, shared breathing, and mindfulness techniques with children in their music classes.

Some teachers highlighted deficiencies in their own college and graduate training. They wished there had been practical courses to prepare them for the classroom, specifically, courses that helped them understand children's musical development and the nature of childhood. Teacher observations of children's innate traits and characteristics were frequent; however, few referenced knowledge of children's natural musicality and spontaneous music and play behaviors. While several teachers recalled such music behaviors with their own children, they said they did not provide similar spontaneous music activities in their music classrooms. Teacher reflections on how children acquire skill, knowledge, and understanding were limited.

In addition, we created a companion website to promote online dialogue as a community resource for sharing thoughts, ideas and teaching practices and for supporting fellow music teachers. Participants will be invited to respond to questions raised in the essays. We welcome responses from teachers who wish to share reflections and teaching experiences and give our assurance of support and encouragement.

Part I: Perspectives

Essay 1, "Born to Be Good," raises the age-old question about the intrinsic nature of goodness versus sinfulness. A host of philosophers, theologians, psychologists, historians, and talk show hosts have debated and splintered each other's positions on matters of good and evil. What we believe about such matters is consequential. As teachers, our deeply held beliefs about the children we teach have an impact on their self-esteem, sense of worth, and confidence. Believing children are innately good gives rise to our best selves and nurtures theirs.

A closer look at the social origins of early humans suggests that we recognize our cooperative nature. Charles Darwin's theory on the process of natural selection was quickly popularized as "survival of the fittest." Some of the "fittest" followers took this to mean the survival of the strongest and the most aggressive. Monikered as "hawks," these followers were secure in their interpretation that history proves them right. "This is mine": so said the first warriors to raid their neighbors, take their land, pillage their treasure, and kidnap their women and children. Superior power speaks to the powerless, "Do you have a flag? You are not a country if you don't have a flag" (Izzard 2010). The whole war-mongering idea caught on about fifteen thousand years ago. Notice that war technology never retreats; it advances from rocks to rockets. Margaret Mead dismissed "it's our nature" theory with knowledge of the many societies, then and now, who did not wage war. In a 1940 essay, Mead declared that "warfare is only an invention [like cooking, marriage, writing, and burial of the dead]—not a biological necessity." More recently, R. Brian Ferguson (2018) in "War Is *Not* a Part of Human Nature" cites anthropological findings and a historical timeline of societies who engaged in collective killing and those who did not.

In winged contrast to the hawks, meet the doves. Social anthropologists give evidence that if you go back far enough, you'll find that hunter-gatherers' survival depended on, well, the kindest. Darwin argued that early humans' social instincts and group organization propelled human evolution. Darwin theorized that natural selection of instincts toward sympathy, belonging in groups, and caring for offspring persisted for millennia.

As the young were cared for, they learned reciprocal caring behaviors and evolved as social beings. We submit that knowledge of our social origins is significant to the present inquiry. By understanding our cultural evolution, we may become secure in the belief that children are born to goodness and so were we.

Essay 2 explores "Music and the Aesthetics of Care." Children's kindness toward others has been observed and documented by teachers, scholars, and researchers (Paley 1999; Ginott 1972; Noddings 2005a, 2005b; Thomas 2015). In *The Kindness Advantage: Cultivating Compassionate and Connected Children* (2018), psychologist Atkins and social worker Salzhauer examine parenting with kindness and teaching children the necessary skills to be compassionate and kind. The authors suggest opportunities for establishing partnerships between parents and teachers to cultivate empathetic and caring children. Accordingly, we have confidence in the intrinsic nature of children's goodness and their propensity for kindness, empathy, and caring; thus, we accept as true that we are called to nurture these qualities and demonstrate them ourselves.

Essay 3 concerns "What Children Need." Cultural anthropologist Ashley Montagu (1989) recognizes "The Neotenous Traits of the Child" in his book *Growing Young*. Montagu asserts there is a broad spectrum of genetically determined characteristics that are too often overlooked in traditional theories of child development and learning. These recognizable traits in children, if supported and valued, contribute to their well-being and eagerness as learners. They include sensitivity, curiosity, wonder, playfulness, imagination, and creativity; knowing, learning, and working; open-mindedness, flexibility, experimentation, and resilience; and enthusiasm, joy, compassion, honesty, and trust. Do you recognize the characteristics cited by Montagu in the children you teach?

In a meaningful and widely read book, *The Irreducible Needs of Children* (2000), pediatrician T. Berry Brazelton and child psychiatrist Stanley I. Greenspan discuss seven irreducible needs of children: nurturing relationships, safety and protection, attention to individual differences, developmentally appropriate experiences, supportive settings with structure and expectations, the need for stable families and communities, and appreciation of cultural identity. In each so-named chapter, the authors provide implications for families, social services, and health systems with recommendations for changes in policies going forward.

Essay 4, "Music and the Spiritual Child," addresses the least acknowledged and least studied attributes of the child we teach. Are there any prevailing associations between children's experience of music and spirituality? From ancient times to the present, suppositions about spirituality have been debated, attested to, and transcribed, particularly in religious texts. Yet, until recently, few researchers have investigated children's spirituality from the child's perspective. Children's spirituality concerns the child's *knowing* beyond their conceptual resources and ability to verbalize as they respond to the extraordinary. According to Michael Polanyi (1958, 1966/2009), tacit knowing is that which cannot be articulated verbally, yet it is the foundation of all knowledge: "They know more than they can tell" (Polanyi 1966/2009, 4). Music's elements and aesthetic qualities, yet unnamable by young children, are nonetheless constant influences in their lives of reality and imagination.

Part II: Pedagogy

Essay 5, "Children's Play with Music," supports the predisposition for and importance of play in children's learning, development, and socialization. Studies of children's play with music indicate that given a free-play setting, preschool children spontaneously explore and create their own music by singing, moving in response to the music they create, and exploring and improvising music with melodic and nonpitched percussion instruments. Studies of teachers' and children's engagement in playfulness are presented. In addition, the significance of children's playful experiences with music at home and school is addressed.

Essay 6, "Wonder-Filled Knowing and Learning," examines music's presence and influence in children's lives from birth through early childhood and adolescence by means of observational research, teachers' narratives, and childhood memories. Furthermore, it is asserted that awareness and understanding of children's innate musical abilities and their prior music experiences shape teachers' decisions about matters of curriculum, instructional strategies, and ecological settings. Children's traits and needs are delineated within favorable music settings and classroom environments, by engaging music experiences, appealing music repertoire, and appropriate boundaries and rules of behavior for classroom music learning and teaching.

Part III: Promises

Essay 7, "Knowing Those Who Teach," explores the external and internal factors that motivate teachers to answer the call to teach music. We suggest that to better understand the children we teach, we must recall our childhood experiences with music, review our beliefs about childhood, and examine how our current teaching practices instill goodness, kindness, musicality, playfulness, spirituality, and wonder in our classrooms.

Essay 8, "Toward a Pedagogy of Hope," proposes ways forward to improve our knowledge and understanding of the children we teach. We suggest a cyclical structure of learning and teaching as an alternative to stage theories of learning. A review of past events and symposia by the National Association for Music Education gives direction toward advancement of learning and teaching music. With children as the focus, we conclude that what we have learned from and about children is analogous to what we have learned about teaching music. What we teach and how we teach emanates from knowing children and ourselves. Each one informs the other. William Wordsworth said it so:

> My heart leaps up when I behold
> A rainbow in the sky:
> So was it when my life began;
> So is it now I am a man;
> So be it when I shall grow old,
> Or let me die!
> The Child is father of the Man;
> And I could wish my days to be
> Bound each to each by natural piety
> ("My Heart Leaps Up" 1802)

Note

1. The Institutional Review Board reviews and monitors all research with human subjects. The study was reviewed by an affiliated university institutional review board to maintain the integrity of the research and protect the rights of the participants. Throughout the text, participants' names were changed to protect their anonymity.

PART I

PERSPECTIVES

ESSAY ONE

Born to Be Good

"He's just like his brothers. They're a bad bunch." This was a warning to me, the new music teacher, from his first-grade teacher. Although she was otherwise a good person, I (Danette Littleton) found that she was unusually harsh in her judgment of her young student, "Artie," and now mine. Why did she believe because his older brothers were troublesome, "bad," the youngest could be no different? I could see that the teacher's attitude toward "Artie" affected the other children's behavior when they came to my music room.

The six-year-old children seemed shy to me. Reticent to participate in singing, playing instruments, or "dancing," they sat and watched me instead. I overheard one little one tell another, "She's going to get in trouble." In other words, they thought I broke the rules of "sit still and be quiet." Before long and with my encouragement and the music activities I offered, the children accepted that this is how we are and what we do when we come for music. Soon, each child eagerly joined in and truly enjoyed making music together. I wrote a Christmas holiday program for them that they performed with enthusiasm. "Artie" sang an angel solo.

This essay introduces a continuous thread that weaves throughout the book—knowing and understanding the children we teach. What we know about children determines how we teach; the learning environments we construct; the music repertoire, content, and skills we provide; and the interdependent teacher-learner relationships we form. The foundation upon which to understand children begins with our belief about their intrinsic goodness. Are they born to be good? Is human nature goodness or wickedness? Can humans achieve enough goodness to overcome predetermined badness? A brief look back at when and from whom this conundrum emerged and why it bears relevance to our voices and visions about teaching children follows.

A cursory review of cultural histories, theosophical theories, and religious dogma reveals conflicting assertions on whether humankind is basically good or evil. Augustine of Hippo's seminal doctrine of original sin prevailed over all other dogma before and after his time. Augustine proclaimed that Adam's sin condemned humanity: all are born in sin, and sin is the cause of evil in the world. Augustine's belief that sins are intrinsic exerted influence on Western philosophy and theology for millennia. During the era of the Enlightenment, opposing views of the nature of humankind were debated. Thomas Hobbes, the pessimist, believed in wickedness. Jean-Jacques Rousseau, the optimist, believed in goodness. Each philosopher had a profound impact on politics, education, and worldview (Locke 1847; Locke did not believe in any innateness, good or evil—he said we were born with a blank slate, *tabula rasa*).

Whether taken literally, symbolically, or unknowingly, this dim view of human nature, particularly of children, calls for scrutiny. This is not to deny that human struggles between good and evil are real or to negate their representations made manifest as hero and villain in fine art, literature, and music. Consider the works of Peter Bruegel, *The Fall of the Rebel Angels*; Dante, *The Divine Comedy*; Carl Orff, *Carmina Burana*; and in popular culture, myths, and fairy tales: *Star Wars*, *Pandora's Box*, and *Hansel and Gretel*. The difference identified here is the dichotomy between predestined sin and evil and the lived experience of the Faustian battle of good and evil.

In the Hobbesian world, it was "war of all against all." However, long after Hobbes died in 1679, a military historian reported startling evidence that servicemen were less, not more, warlike. US Army lieutenant colonel Samuel Marshall was asked to interview World War II soldiers for action details after a four-day battle on Makin Island in the Pacific. He was shocked to find that only thirty-eight of three hundred men had fired their weapons. Subsequently, Marshall interviewed hundreds more World War II soldiers in Europe and the Pacific. In 1947, his findings published in *Men Against Fire: The Problem of Battle Command* (1947/2000), reported that only 15 percent had fired at the enemy during combat. Similar findings showed that after the Civil War Battle of Gettysburg in 1863, 90 percent of the thousands of muskets recovered from the battlefields were fully loaded. Marshall concluded that the average and normally healthy individual in war, starting with the Greeks at Troy, had a powerful instinct against killing. In a letter home, British General Montgomery wrote, "The trouble with our British boys is that they are not killers by nature" (Bregman 2019, 83). Historians and archeologists continued to explore the phenomenon that soldiers were trying not to kill the enemy.

In *Humankind: A Hopeful History* (2019) Bregman guides the reader to a new view of humanity through an impressive study of scientists in an array of different fields. For example, physician and sociologist Nicholas Christakis's (2019) vision of human beings "holds that people are, and should be, united by our common humanity. And this commonality originates in our shared evolution. It is written in our genes" (xx). Evolutionary anthropologist Brian Hare's studies (2017, 2020) concluded that human survival depended on "the friendliest." Hare and Vanessa Woods (2020) explained that "what allowed us to thrive while other humans went extinct was a kind of cognitive superpower: a particular type of friendliness called cooperative communication" (xxiv). This gave us the possibilities to work together on shared goals, communities, and trade routes, and create rock and cave paintings: "We not only imitated life, but we also imagined and portrayed mythical creatures" (xxiv). Friendships and friendliness, sharing, creating, and imagining are qualities and traits that we observe in modern children that must be encouraged at school and at play.

Scientific evidence suggests that we reject what Augustine and Hobbes think of us and embrace *the better angels of our nature*. When Abraham Lincoln gave his First Inaugural Address, seven Southern states had already seceded from the Union. President Lincoln said, "The mystic chords of memory, stretching from every battlefield and patriot grave to every heart and hearth-stone, all over this broad land, will yet swell the chorus of the Union, when again touched, as surely they will be, by the better angels of our nature." Lincoln's words are often called for in times of despair, but when we look into the eyes of children the brightness of better angels and the light of goodness shines back at us, and our hopefulness is restored.

In *Born to Be Good: The Science of a Meaningful Life* (2009), Dacher Keltner studied the evolution of the outward manifestation of goodness. He wrote, "Cooperation, kindness, and virtue are embodied in observable acts—facial muscle movements, brief vocalizations, ways of moving the hands or positioning the body, patterns of gaze activity—that are signals detectable to the ordinary eye" (72). In addition, Keltner said that "scientific studies illuminate this new swath of human design, and that [it] will lend credence to Darwin's insight about the origin of human goodness: that it is rooted in our emotions, and that these social instincts [for goodness] may be stronger than those of any other instinct or motive" (73). It begins in infancy.

Research and on-site observations by teachers confirm that very young children exhibit characteristics of cooperation, sharing, and fairness. Vivian

Paley (1991, 1993, 2009), a pioneering teacher and author, mentored generations of teachers of young children. She was possibly the only kindergarten teacher to receive a MacDonald Foundation "Genius" award. Her contribution to child development is exemplary and extensive. In each of her thirteen books, and in her articles and lectures, she reveals children's behaviors of goodness and fairness, and through methods of storytelling and playacting she guides them to their best selves and care for others.

You Can't Say You Can't Play (1993) is the book title for a rule she established to teach her kindergarten children about rejection and hurt feelings. As a master teacher researcher, she listened to children and kept a journal to reflect and fine-tune her approach.

The Boy Who Would Be a Helicopter: The Uses of Storytelling in the Classroom (1991) is about a lonely boy, Jason, who remained secluded in his own world, unwilling to let his classmates inside. For most of the school year, Jason continued to be isolated within his invented helicopter stories. A particular situation caught his attention: when "someone" needed a ride home from school, he created a scenario to solve the problem. Jason said that he had a three-seater helicopter that would carry them home. "Everyone is going to hold everyone's hand." Ms. Paley explains that in Jason's story, a child is lost at school, but his helicopter will rescue them. "The ultimate fear and loss, Jason tells us, is separation" (147). Jason's helicopter, his friend, helped him make other friends.

Paley (1990) tells us, "We must become aware of the essential loneliness of each child. Our classrooms, at all levels, must look more like happy families and secure homes, the kind in which all family members can tell their private stories, knowing they will be listened to with affection and respect" (147). We, like Ms. Paley, must ask, "What does it feel like to be a teacher?" and more importantly, "What does it feel like to be a child?"

In *The Kindness of Children* (2009) written upon her retirement, she reflects on thirty-seven years of listening to, observing, and teaching young children. Ms. Paley recalls, "Children are more often kind to each other than unkind. The early instinct to help someone is powerful" (129). In closing, she wrote, "The unkind voices that surround us are loud and shrill, demanding our thoughtful and truthful attention. All the more reason to listen for the soft breath of friendship and carry our reassuring stories above the din" (129).

The evidence and perspectives cited here are the lintel stones upon which to construct a "new view" of the children we teach. What would our music classrooms be like if we realized and acted on belief in the innate goodness of children? Would we seek to understand children's disorderly behaviors and help them with self-control strategies? Would we be more likely to welcome their presence with pleasure? Would we show true enjoyment when making music with them? Would we smile more?[1]

Consider two classroom scenarios where you are, alternatively, a kindergarten child and a music teacher. As a young child, what were you like in music class: timid and shy, unsettled and unruly, or confident and assertive? Did you feel welcomed and included? What music activities were your favorites? What do you remember about your music teacher?

Now, imagine exchanging roles. What are you like now as a music teacher? What are your most successful music activities with children? How do you respond to children's positive and/or negative behaviors during music-making activities? How do you bring out the goodness in children? As you think about the complexity of the moment-to-moment engagement, interactions, and interruptions, what do you most want to know about teaching children music? Consider yourself in each of these scenarios. What are your thoughts and recollections? With these questions as guides, create a screenplay featuring you as the child and you as the teacher in an imaginary music class. We invite you to share your ideas and reflections through our online community journal (www.knowingthechildrenweteach.com).

Alice's Perspective
Alice has been teaching in New York City public schools for ten years. One of her first jobs was in a Title I, low-income school in Brooklyn. She described a community of students whose lives were impacted by homelessness and violence. Many children did not have access to regular meals and often exhibited angry and disruptive behaviors. She talked about using percussion as an outlet for the children to release emotion. Mostly, she spoke about compassion, connection, and caring: "When you become a teacher, you become family to these kids."

Scholar, researcher, and anthropologist Ellen Dissanayake (2000) stated that the human biological need to seek connection in relationships results in a mutuality characterized by "having the same feelings one for the other," bonds that tie us together (19). Alice was able to look beyond her students' anger and disruption to show compassion for them. Becoming family means being connected through bonds of love and mutuality.

A major theme emerging from the data showed that many children were purposely seeking understanding and attention. They wanted to be known as individuals, to be seen and heard.

Kayla's Perspective
Kayla, an orchestra teacher, described how a frustrated middle school student who lacked self-confidence and was always comparing herself to others needed

kindness, compassion, and attention. Kayla spoke about taking the time after class to allow her to "be seen" and understood. The eighth grader regularly compared herself to a high-achieving classmate. She was very tough on herself. Kayla said, "Hey, I see you. I can tell how much you are working; I can tell how much you are practicing." The student later confided, "It felt really important to be seen like that." In the days leading up to performance, Kayla said that her students' musicality and artistry were refined: "[They] really get in the zone."

Teaching is powerful when students interpret the music they perform by merging creative and technical elements. Kayla said, "I step back and let students take control. Say as little as possible . . . then let them do it." She explained that she encouraged students to reflect on their experience and figure out how to revise and improve by taking agency throughout the process. "Put learning in their hands—with my guidance." Kayla shared that she learned to conduct her classroom by experience, not from a college class or manual but by building relationships. She concluded, "[I let] the students tell me how they want to be taught."

Tara's Perspective
Similarly, Tara, an elementary school teacher, spoke about a second grader with disruptive and defiant behavior in the classroom. She described how making connections outside the classroom, like greeting the child at morning drop-off, and establishing a relationship made the child feel understood. Dissanayake (2000) contended that the human need for connection and understanding are the "emotional food and warmth" of relationships. Through kind interactions during music making, Tara recognized and responded to the child's need for connection and understanding. She individualized classroom activities to allow him to express himself through drawing during class. Many children need outlets for their powerful emotions.

Trevor's Perspective
Trevor, an elementary and middle school general music and band teacher of nine years, recalled a particular disruptive student in his band sessions. However, Trevor noted that along with the distractions, the child brought a wonderful sense of comedy, lightheartedness, and fun to the ensemble. Trevor found ways to harness this energy and foster a band experience that made time for fun and enjoyment.

Jordan's Perspective
Jordan shared an experience with a fourth grade boy who was energetic and often disruptive in her music class. It began with a music composition activity in which the children were asked to represent their emotions as well as those of their peers. This once unruly child excelled at the activity and was gratified to be seen and

heard by the teacher and his classmates. Jordan remembered, "A music-making experience [helped] this child to show his intuitive self, and to show his peers that he's really in tune with himself and others, rather than always being seen as the disrupter." Engagement with music and an outlet for expression and understanding brought out the best in this good child.

Morgan's Perspective
Morgan is a professional clarinetist who teaches music in the South Bronx. In addition, she advises a student group, Gender Sexuality Alliance Club. She begins in response to a question about student behavior, "I don't describe actions as disruptive, per se."

By way of explaining, Morgan introduces KK, a senior student in the Gender Sexuality Alliance Club and music classes who spends his free periods in her classroom. KK always shows a wide range of emotions. He is emotionally transparent and shows how he feels through dress and makeup. Morgan realizes that when KK puts on a hood, it is a sign that means he needs personal space and to physically shut off. She acknowledges the difficult lives of her students, their emotional disturbances, and the baggage and poverty cycles that keep them isolated. "They've never even been to Manhattan." She takes them on trips for new experiences, like attending their first live show performance. "I feel like they can finally breathe." When asked what she learned about teaching, from teaching, Morgan replied without hesitation, "Never treat students as subordinates, but with mutual respect as equals, friends, whole beings." She adds that

> blame doesn't work in the classroom. We are not our behaviors. . . . Seek to understand the lived experience of your students and those of your own. There's a story and reasoning for every action and reaction. Give students the benefit of the doubt and give yourself the benefit of the doubt with kindness and compassion—the best version of ourselves.

Just as we must be aware of children's emotions, their need for connection and desire for acknowledgment, we must also be conscious of how our expressions impact the children in our classrooms. Science and common sense confirm that what children hear in our words and see in our demeanor, facial expressions, and gestures convey our minute-to-minute thoughts and feelings as we interact with them. Detailed studies of human emotion expressed through facial images were first conducted by Charles Darwin. He collected and analyzed over one hundred photographs of actors portraying different emotions (Keltner 2009, 17). Keltner (2009) wrote that Darwin proposed as many as sixteen positive emotions and that "these kinds of data led Darwin to a rich portrayal, the most detailed ever achieved, of human emotional expression" and that his "observations are a poetic periodic chart of how emotions are expressed, the embodied signatures of brief subjective states" (18).

One hundred years after Darwin's work on emotions, scientist Paul Ekman (1993) designed a way to measure emotion through the Facial Action Coding System. His methodology allowed researchers to identify and analyze facial expression as it "occurs in the seamless flow of social interaction" (32). Ekman brought attention to Darwin's insight that the origin of human goodness is rooted in our emotions and that these social instincts may be stronger than those of any other instinct or motive (Ekman 1993, 73). Ekman's lifetime work on facial expression and emotion and nonverbal communication generated a new field of scientific inquiry, *affective neuroscience*. He writes, "The [positive] emotions that I have been so fortunate to capture in my lab, just for a fragile, fleeting instant, have their evolutionary provenance in a reverence and respect for others" (Ekman 1993, 268). We are wired for goodness.

Teachers like these model goodness and care for their students. Alice is like family to her students. Kayla takes time for a student who needs compassion and understanding. Tara finds a way to help a child who needs a positive outlet for his emotions. Trevor refuses to label disruptive behavior "bad"; rather he incorporates his student's sense of fun and lightheartedness appropriately within the band community. Jordan brings out the best in an attention-seeking child through music as a means of self-expression and a tool for understanding the child's needs. Morgan shares her journey teaching troubled students. For them, she establishes a democratic classroom that depends on her students' cooperation and helps them create their own standards and class rules. Theirs is a learning environment of mutual respect, compassion, and understanding.

Teaching is demanding and complex. Nevertheless, it is our internal resources of mind and spirit that enable us to understand and be understood. In no more than a passing moment, our interaction with children through music is life changing. We are summoned to see that goodness in children is innate. Goodness is their birthright, and ours. As we interact with children, they intuit what they mean to us. The child we see, sees us.

Note

1. From Lin-Manuel Miranda, *Hamilton: An American Musical*. "Talk less. Smile more" is wise counsel for teachers, too.

ESSAY TWO

Music and the Aesthetics of Care

This essay explores children's propensity toward kindness and shows how to recognize, support, and encourage kind behaviors—theirs and ours. Yolanda disliked her fourth-grade classmates, and they disliked her (she didn't like me, either). All children in this school came from the same tough neighborhood, where kindness meant weakness and fights were common. After one particularly difficult incident involving Yolanda in my music class, I asked her to come by after school to talk about what happened. She was sullen and refused to talk, until I asked what music she liked.

"Mariah Carey."
"Do you have a favorite song?"
"'Hero.'"
"I like that one too. Would you sing it for me?"

Surprisingly, she did, just like Mariah Carey. I asked if she'd allow me to make a video so she could see and hear herself singing. Afterward, she was harsh with self-criticism and defeat. "Do you want to know what I heard?" As she accepted my encouragement and musical guidance, her confidence swelled. She smiled and asked if I would give her more "singing lessons." As she gained confidence, I asked if she would sing for her classmates. What happened next was transformative for Yolanda and for me and her classmates. Like one of those "Got Talent" TV shows, the audience was skeptical—until she started to sing. The cheers and applause went straight to Yolanda's heart. She found the hero in herself (Littleton 2015).

Transformation, like Yolanda's, only comes about from within; it cannot be taught. Like nested Russian dolls, children have an outward appearance of identity that others see. Further inside and less revealed are traits of personality and character. Hidden at the core of identity is the deeply held knowledge children keep to themselves. How, then, does a teacher permeate layers of children's individuality with sensitivity and respect? As an example, consider the emotional aspects and classroom conditions that brought about change in an angry girl and her unfriendly classmates.

Given that the classroom was inhospitable due to the emotions generated by a hostile incident, Yolanda needed a private, safe space to settle down. I asked if she would come back after school. In most situations like this, I try to find out what caused the problem. I ask, "Can I help?" or "What are you going through?" However, some students do not respond to deeply personal questions. My aim that day was to convey empathy and respect for Yolanda, to (a) observe and listen to her with compassionate concern; (b) give her time to speak; (c) ask a nonintimidating question, "What music do you like?"; (d) bring about a relationship of care, if only for a few minutes; (e) meet Yolanda as an equal person; and finally (f) keep an open mind in difficult situations and help the angry child and her taunting classmates keep an open mind too.

Yolanda's identification with her song reminds me of a story about how an African tribe bestows a song that identifies a child from birth until the end of life. When a woman knows she's having a baby, she leaves the village with family and friends and goes into the wilderness to pray and meditate until they hear the song of the unborn child. They return to the village and teach the child's song to the community. Again, when the child is born, the villagers gather and sing the baby's song to her. And so it goes. Throughout the child's lifetime, from childhood to initiation passage to adulthood and at her wedding, the people sing her song. As her life ends, family and friends gather at her bedside, just as they did at her birth, and for the last time they sing her song as it lifts her soul away to the next life. If at any time in life she commits some wrongdoing, the community forms a circle around her and sings to remind her of her true self. They embrace her with love and compassion instead of rejection and punishment (Cohen 2019).

There is a connection from the African story to Yolanda's story. Instead of the villagers' rituals of bestowing the song, Yolanda chose a song of her own. Like the village child, Yolanda's song expressed her individuality, and somewhat like the villagers, her classmates showed acceptance and uplifted her spirit (Villalpando 2021). These stories demonstrate the fundamental quality of kindness that we can make real for the children we teach. In her book *Compassionate Music Teaching*, Karin Hendricks (2018) suggests that music teachers can "utilize music and music learning spaces as a means of encouraging connection, sensitivity and kindness" (62). However, in the absence of the ethics of care, feelings are unacknowledged and children suffer.

Maya's Perspective
Maya, a teacher-participant, is an experienced music educator with children, pre-K to sixth grade. Currently, as a college educator, she trains future music teachers. Maya recalled a hurtful experience from her childhood when a general music teacher embarrassed her in front of the class and eroded her confidence. She remembers being forced to sing by herself while facing her classmates. When her voice cracked, everyone laughed at her. Looking back, she says "it was a wholly unfulfilling experience." For Maya, a climate of support and an understanding teacher were missing that day.

LaVerne's Perspective
In a recent interview with LaVerne, a great grandmother, she vividly recalled,

> When I was about eight years old, the church choir leader wanted to start a children's choir. Our Sunday school teacher told us we should join. At the first time to practice, Bob Stubblefield, the choir director, stopped and yelled, "Who's that growling!" Well, he started us singing again. Then, he stopped, looked straight at me, and pointed his finger. I got up, left right then, and never went back!

Gabriela's Perspective
In another interview, Gabriela shared her experiences as a high school vocal major at a school for the performing arts.

> The worst was with adjunct faculty, who were sometime-performers and who should not have been teachers. One of them was emotionally abusive to kids who "couldn't get it," especially when they were singing in a language they didn't know. He was all about working on technique, and even that failed. Music was more accessible to me. I knew I was a better singer, but I didn't want others to feel that. Instead, I became a scapegoat. It became a hostile environment that the teacher ignored. My attachment to the emotionality of singing was hindered and suppressed by his objectivity and dismissal of me. Notes versus expression. He didn't understand that I just wanted to grow.

We learned of her musical background as Gabriela told us of her experience as a choral singer from age eight to fourteen:

> I've always had high expectations for myself from the time I sang in the Children's Festival Chorus. Most memorable was the Lord's Prayer in Hebrew by an American composer, modern, emotional gravity. I always wanted to perform it again. I remember the fun of singing as a group. There was a call-and-response song, in Swahili, that we could spontaneously sing anywhere, anytime. It is a powerful collective memory.

Continuing in her own words, Gabriela expressed what solo singing means to her:

> Musically, I am high-strung, affectively sensitive, with high expectations of my singing. I was about twelve or thirteen when I had five solos in *Lessons and Carols*. Halfway through "Once in David's Royal City," I started choking. It must have been the dusty air. I don't know; it had never happened before. I couldn't finish and started crying (the people around me were not very nice about it). Next, I was to sing a duet arranged by British organist Alistair Stout. It was melodically complex, had a very Herbert Howells kind of vibe. I was fine—crying may have helped—by the last verse my voice was back! At the last verse, I reached the high G or A, really, kinda, fabulously. It was a powerful feeling. I've only felt that two times. I was fifteen or so by the next time. It was a performance of the Couperin "Tenebres" for two voices. I sang the upper descant; and in a moment, I let go to some kind of clarity of sound. I haven't had that clarity of sound since. Just floating up in the nanosphere, easily, just so easily. It's quite personal to me to be that audibly clear. I pride myself on clarity. I think it's audibly clear to others, that exposed sound.

Our voice is our identity as we speak and sing. Through our voice, we express our mood and feelings as we communicate with others. Graham Welch (2012), in *The Benefits of Singing for Children*, writes that

> singing can allow us to feel better about ourselves and about the world around us. From pre-birth, our earliest auditory experiences are biased towards the human voice, principally from first hearing our mother's voice inside the womb. All voice use, including singing, is interwoven with core emotional states that are central to the human condition, such as joy and sadness. (3)

Welch identifies the following psychological, social, musical, and educational advantages of the power of singing: what singing means, identity, positive self-concept, expressing feelings; communication with others, belonging, social inclusion, group identity; intellectual understanding of music;

individual musical repertoire as a listener, performer, or both; and knowledge of and about music and music cultures throughout the world.

Vocalization as communication is universal in birds, whales, and humans. There is evidence that music or singing may have evolved in humans before language did. Levitin, in *This Is Your Brain on Music* (2006), argues that "music may be the activity that prepared our pre-human ancestors for speech communication" and that "singing . . . might have helped our species to refine motor skills, paving the way for the development of the exquisitely fine muscle control required for vocal . . . speech" (260). Humans' spoken languages have identifiable qualities in tone, rhythm, phrasing, and structure. Individual human voices have such unique characteristics that we can easily recognize the voices of those we know.

The child's voice, spoken or sung, is fundamental to that child's identity of knowing and being known. Singing experience in childhood, positive or negative, has a long-term impact on children's self-esteem and musical development. Knight (2010) studied how adverse childhood singing experiences contributed to adults becoming nonsingers. He concluded that negative self-perception affected their lives from personal and sociocultural perspectives.

Laura's Perspective
One of the teacher-participants in his study, Laura, remembered,

> Then in grade six, I stood up to sing it and she told me to sit down, that I couldn't sing. Well, I was devastated. . . . I'm sure I wanted to cry. Of course, you came home, it was no good of telling your parents at the time that something like this had happened to you. And she was such a powerful person in the community. It stayed with me for so long. It was so degrading at the time. Even in high school, if there was anything to do with music, I hated music . . . I didn't learn it. I couldn't learn it, as I thought . . . I'm sure that [incident] affected [my involvement with music] in a lot of ways. Maybe she just didn't have the knowledge and it didn't come to her, "I am doing something that's going to affect this child for most of her life." That's probably the way it was.

Even the great master cellist Pablo Casals was subjected to ill treatment by a music professor. At eighteen, he left Spain to study at the Conservatoire in Belgium, famous for its strings program. After other students had played, the professor addressed Casals: "So! You must be the little Spaniard the director has been telling me all about." The professor continued to grill young Casals about repertoire: "Well, it seems our little Spaniard can play everything! He must be quite amazing!" The students all laughed at the sarcasm. He continued, "Perhaps you will honor us with your playing. I'm sure we'll hear something unbelievable from this young man who can play everything." More laughter as he borrowed a cello from one of the students. Then he started to play. The room fell silent.

"Will you please come to my office?" the teacher then asked politely. "Young man, I can tell that you have a very special talent. If you study here and agree to be in my class, I can promise you that you will be awarded the First Prize of the Conservatoire. It is hardly according to the rules that I should tell you this now—but I will give you my word." Casals, still angry, replied, "You were rude to me, sir. You ridiculed me in front of your pupils. I do not wish to remain here one second longer." The professor stood up and opened the door (Lloyd Webber 1985, 24–25).

When children are admonished by their choir director or classroom music teacher to "mouth the words" or "pretend to sing," children's essence of being is deeply wounded. Adults do not forget the embarrassment they felt as a child wrongly labeled "nonsinger" or "monotone." Schei and Schei (2017) studied the impact of "voice shaming," when a child internalizes inadequacy following negative interactions with authority figures like parents and teachers. As music teachers, we must be keenly aware of our power to uplift young singers rather than cause them harm with damaging words and judgments. As music teachers, we are called to show kindness and understanding of the children we teach. We want loving messages to remain with children throughout their lives. If we care for children's well-being first, musical skills, knowledge, and joy of music and singing will follow.

In *Art and Intimacy: How the Arts Began* (2000), Ellen Dissanayake describes the human need for connection: "Mutuality with other individuals and belonging to a group are as necessary to human life as food and warmth" (51). Morgan, introduced in the previous essay, embodies mutuality as she creates safe spaces, inside and outside her classroom, where her students feel accepted and cared for. She draws on personal experiences to connect with students struggling with their identities. Her egalitarian music classroom is guided by the principle that students are responsible for the rules and norms for behaviors in her classes. Morgan regards her students as co-learners, not subordinates. She works to connect with her students and creates a means for them to connect with each other. Her openness, vulnerability, and consideration for her students are hallmarks of kindness.

In their book *The Kindness Advantage: Cultivating Compassionate and Connected Children* (2018), psychologist Atkins and social worker Salzhauer define the fundamental attributes of kindness as acceptance, commitment, connection, giving, nurturing, observing, questioning, being yourself, and empathizing. Shane, one of our participants, is an experienced music teacher who found his way to teaching through performing. He did not study music education before he began teaching but learned to teach *by* teaching. "Being a parent helped me to be a better teacher." He explained that parenting his children with autism, dyslexia, and ADHD gave him a special perspective on teaching: "Working with them, raising them, loving them, has really helped me to better understand [my students]." Subsequently, Shane's kindness and love for his children were conveyed to his students. Atkins and Salzhauer (2018) say, "Our emotional responses [are] an important part of what makes us human and connects us with others so that we can see the world through their eyes" (36).

Nel Noddings, in *The Challenge of Care in Schools: An Alternative Approach to Education* (2005a) explains that "an ethic of care embodies a relational view of caring; that is, when I speak of caring, my emphasis is on the relation containing [the one who cares] and the cared-for." She continues, "Caring is a way of being in relation, not a specific set of behaviors" (17). Noddings makes clear that an ethics of care begins with the responsibility of self-care that enables teachers to model for students how to care in relation to others. Importantly, Noddings identifies dialogue, practice, and confirmation as major components of a moral education. She writes, "Dialogue is open-ended. Dialogue is a common search for understanding, empathy, or appreciation. It can be playful or serious, logical, or imaginative, goal or process orientated, but it is always a genuine quest for something undetermined at the beginning" (23). Practice involves providing opportunities for our students to gain skills in caregiving, whereas confirmation of caring involves acts of affirming and encouraging the best in others. "When we confirm someone, we spot a better self and encourage its development. We can only do this if we know the other well enough to see what he or she is trying to become" (25).

To teach is to be in a relationship that connects self to other.

Jack's Perspective
Jack, another of our teacher-participants, spoke about his use of music to encourage kindness and empathy. He said,

> I learned in school that teaching people is far more important than the subject matter that you teach; you can't do one without the other. You must remember that that 95 percent of the facts and details and minutiae that students learn in school is forgotten and not utilized; but learning how to be good people, learning how to be good citizens, learning how to socialize, learning how to express their emotions in a positive way, learning how to be members of a community—

all of these are things that they will take with them. So, you try to teach them how to be good people, how to be active learners, how to inspire them to think critically, and to use their experiences in school towards all the aspects of their lives. The subject matter that you teach is merely a vehicle through which you help young people grow. Showing empathy, kindness, and understanding is what makes it possible for them to say, "Okay, this is an individual, who cares about me as a person, invested in me as a person, who's going to teach me stuff." Maybe that disruptive youngster has not had an opportunity to experience empathy or develop coping skills.

Jack realized that finding the source and reason for negative behavior helps him help his students.

Melody's Perspective
Melody, a young teacher who is beginning her career and completing her master's degree, spoke about the lack of empathy and understanding as the root cause of disruptive behavior. She told us about a recent experience with a student, Sam. She recalled,

> In my first few encounters with Sam, he was full of joy and excitement for music. Always willing to participate in our activities and facilitate classmates and friends when necessary. With that, when the first marking period came around, I was confident in awarding him a [grade of] four out of five. Sam's classroom teacher approached me after viewing the grades and questioned my decision.

Melody went on to say that the classroom teacher highlighted Sam's disruptive behavior in her class and insisted, despite Melody's disagreement, that she lower Sam's music grade. After this encounter, Melody said there was a big change in Sam. He became "the most disruptive and angry student I had encountered thus far. He would scream and yell, throw rhythm sticks and other materials, and do just about anything to be off task. Since then, Sam has been this disruptive and distracting student, unwilling to participate, or even sit in the circle with his peers for music." Melody struggled to understand why Sam was labeled as a "bad kid" in his general classroom but responded so well in his music class. She said, "I am undoubtedly questioning my abilities as a teacher and facilitator to each student's learning needs. I hope that in the coming weeks I can understand what change occurred." Instead of labeling Sam or placing blame on him or the general classroom teacher, Melody approached the situation with steadfast understanding.

Throughout this essay we explored how children use singing as a means of self-expression and identity and we showed how they enjoy singing alone and with others and belonging to a choral performing group. By the preteen and teen years, childhood yields to developmental changes, social and peer influences, and individuation. It is a time in life when music becomes a significant presence in the lives of adolescents. It is a time when many young songwriters, like John Lennon and Paul McCartney, begin to write and perform.

The impetus for musical identity is linked to maturation and independence. During adolescence, popular music accompanies teens in their search for identity and emotional agency. Musical preferences and involvement in musical activities are prominent in the transition from parental protection and guidance to self-determination and autonomy.

Despite the attention given to music that expresses defiance of authority, Zillmann and Gan (1997) suggest that elements of youth music are of considerable variance and that their music is difficult to categorize "due to the complexity and multidimensionality of the musical products to be classified" (165). Less known or studied is that adolescents consume most of their music outside school and in solitude. "Adolescent music is created, for the most part, by adolescents" (Zillmann and Gan 1997, 163).

John Kratus (2016) explains that songwriting classes connect students' out-of-school music interests with their in-school music learning. He offers the following goals: (1) immersing students in creating and performing in a style that is meaningful to them; (2) fulfilling their interest in learning fretted, keyboard, or electronic instruments; (3) addressing social and psychological needs; and (4) providing a musical skill that lasts a lifetime. The value of teaching songwriting places the focus on the students' musical ideas, not the teacher's.

Further research studies show that songwriting is a therapeutic means to help children cope with grief, loss, transition, homelessness, and abuse (Dalton and Krout 2005; Fairchild and McFerran 2019; Fiore 2016; Roberts 2006). Songwriting is not widely embraced in the school music curriculum, except when schools employ external teachers or organizations that offer programs to engage children in songwriting. Beth and Scott Bierko are musicians, arts educators, and singer-songwriters who provide music workshops in schools ("Workshops and Residencies" n.d.). Their programs focus on social-emotional learning, mindfulness, and yoga to empower children in expressing themselves through music and songwriting. In past years, they visited my (Meryl Sole) daughters' elementary school and worked with the children to write original songs that illustrate the school norms: "be here, be safe, be honest, care for self and others, and let go and move on." In my oldest daughter's fifth-grade class, they composed a song called "I Believe in Kindness," expressing a message of compassion and self-care.

Based in Austin, Texas, the Kindness Campaign offers songwriting as a channel for children for self-expression as they compose original songs, "to create positive, accessible tools to build emotional health at home and in the classroom" (Villalpando 2021).

Daisy's Perspective

We invited singer-songwriter Daisy Annabelle ("Daisy Anabelle" n.d.) to describe her process of songwriting from childhood as she learned to write and perform her own songs. Daisy grew up in a musical family. Her mother is an artist and teacher, and her father is a professional musician, educator, and songwriter who continues to serve as her musical mentor. As an adolescent, she recalls songwriting, "like having this encouragement, the support system, to know how to express yourself and create something of your own right."

Daisy, who lost her grandmother when she was thirteen years old, spoke of how writing a song helped her grieve her loss. She explained, "I felt that incredible healing sense of feeling better in a time where it felt like I would never feel better again." Using songwriting to cope and heal remained into adulthood: "Ever since then every difficult thing, even just difficult or annoying days, I wanted to write a song, because it makes me feel better." For Daisy, songwriting is a therapeutic outlet for emotion and a tool for processing experience.

Her passion for creating music, introduced and nurtured by her family, was not part of her formal education. She believed that a songwriting class in school might have enhanced her experience of music making and creativity. While teaching a songwriting class is intimidating for teachers without experience or training opportunities, the rewards for students are many when they share original songs with inspiration, confidence, openness, and honesty.

How, then, might music teachers acquire the skills and confidence necessary to explore songwriting with children? Consider Modern Band and Little Kids Rock, which afford children opportunities to learn to play popular instruments like guitar, bass, drums, ukulele, and write songs. These programs "bring innovative and inclusive music education to students. Using popular music styles like rock, pop, rap, and Latin, our teachers build music programs that are as diverse as the kids they serve" ("Little Kids Rock" n.d.).

Bryan Powell, director of higher education at Little Kids Rock, observed that music teachers were usually students who achieved success in band, orchestra, and chorus programs with emphasis on instrumental and vocal proficiency. However, instruction for composing and songwriting is limited or not offered. When teachers "get into the school system, they don't facilitate songwriting in their classroom because they feel unprepared."

Randles (2018) examined the experiences of music teachers who participated in Modern Band workshops through Little Kids Rock. His study revealed only 32 percent of teachers reported that their students composed original songs. Activities focused on playing instruments instead of using them for songwriting, as teachers showed a lack of confidence in using technology or working with digital music software. Randles concluded, if students are going to compose original songs, then their teachers need experience in composing original songs. Unfortunately, courses where future teachers learn to write original songs as a part of their teacher preparation are not currently the norm.

It is never too late for middle, high school, or even college music students to learn songwriting; however, we submit that improvising and composing songs best begins with young children. Powell of Little Kids Rock concurred: "I think the richest environment for songwriting is with the little ones, because they're going to be the most open to it. They're doing it, you know, in their musical life outside of the classroom as well."

Music teachers understand children's natural impetus for spontaneous song and music making. In a classroom with three-year-old children, the music teacher (Danette Littleton) initiated a one-to-one singing activity. Pointing to pictures in a storybook, she asked a little girl, "Would you sing a song for them?" Of course, the child began to sing about the pictures, without hesitation or any lack of confidence, in creating an original story-song with melodic and rhythmic structure. If children are invited to play freely and spontaneously as music makers, then, as teens, they may be likely to engage in self-initiated songwriting, composing, or playing an instrument.

Children are natural song makers; however, despite their unique abilities in creating spontaneous songs, they are rarely afforded opportunities for notating or recording their songs. In their support, let us rethink our strategies to facilitate children's impetus for making a world of music all their own.

The Aesthetics of Care asks us to seek the musical and personal identity of each child through compassionate teaching, kindness, and heartfelt commitment to their well-being.

> We must educate our young children in the practice of compassion on a worldwide scale. Teachers and parents can instill in children real, warm-hearted human values to tremendous benefit. We need a transformation in commitment to the universal values of compassion and love.
>
> —The Dalai Lama (2022)

ESSAY THREE

What Children Need

In the previous essay, "Music and the Aesthetics of Care," we demonstrated that kind and compassionate teaching are vitally important to children's musical identity and personal well-being. This essay explores the symbiosis of children's basic needs and innate traits with their experience of music.

First, we turn our attention to the fundamental needs of children. In *The Irreducible Needs of Children: What Every Child Must Have to Grow, Learn, and Flourish* (2009), the authors, pediatrician Berry Brazelton and child psychiatrist Stanley Greenspan, provide seven principles that guide our inquiry, stating that children need (1) nurturing relationships; (2) physical protection and safety; (3) experiences attuned to individual differences; (4) developmentally appropriate experiences; (5) limitations, expectations, and structure; (6) stable supportive communities and cultural continuity; and (7) protection for the future.

When children's needs are unmet, they cannot grow, learn, and thrive; often they are at risk for negativism, rebellion, and violence or fear, anxiety, and passivity. Brazelton and Greenspan assert that the need for ongoing nurturing from birth is commonly understood, but actual practices and environments tend toward the impersonal. Caregivers, daycare providers, and teachers who recognize and provide for the needs of children contribute to their happy and healthy childhoods.

What Children Need

We invited the teacher-participants to respond to questions about nurturing and supporting children, attention to individual differences, providing for developmentally appropriate experiences with music, and creating an environment of safety and acceptance. The following excerpts are from teachers' video interviews.

Nurturing Relationships

Alice's Perspective

Alice described the cumulative needs of her students, those who were hungry, homeless, and experienced lives of trauma. She recognized their needs for understanding, support, and nurturing. "As their music teacher, I had the space, and I had the platform to inspire these kids just to become better human beings. I did that through music. We did a lot of percussion. Lots of singing. I built my lessons based on what my kids liked so that it was a really great experience—still is."

Abigail's Perspective

Abigail spoke about children's need for belonging and acceptance. She observed that participating in musical theater allowed students to be vulnerable and open with their peers. "Expressing thoughts and feelings through the world of music and singing have been incredibly powerful." Abigail knew the importance of being attuned to individual students. "I learned to listen to them and watch them. I used my observation skills to find out what they needed, socially and musically, so that information [and knowledge] could guide my pedagogy and curriculum."

Bennett's Perspective

Bennett discovered the importance of connecting with students and understanding their interests and needs. He learned to

> connect with the human being. Have conversations with students about what's important to them and understand their goals—not just view them as a participant in the music program. Something I was never taught to consider when I was in school [college]. It was all about [treating] students in your ensemble as if they were contributing cogs in the overall machine. Student-as-participant to the overall thing, not as an individual. My students had their own preferences. It sounds so obvious now when I say it out loud, but it's a connection that I found valuable and stayed with me all these years of teaching.

Continuing, Bennett reminded us of what many teachers know—that music provides a place for belonging. The band program was a place "for those who did not have a place in school where they felt they could express themselves, a place where they were accepted for who they are. Having sympathy, understanding, and getting to know each student [brings about] the ability to meet each child's needs." Bennett extended his care for students by partnering with their parents. "I realize that raising a teenager today is challenging. You know we're in this together, we're partners [making] an investment for your daughter and son." Bennett spoke of creating a community within the band where students are connected and committed to each other. "All the work we've done and shared with our parents expresses our music together."

Individual Differences and Inclusion
Jordan's Perspective
Jordan used her talent and experience as a singer-songwriter to approach her students as individuals, to lift them up. "To me songwriting was one of the most healing and grounding things in my life." When students presented their songs to the class, she discovered the importance of social emotional learning—how we listen and how we respond to each other. It is the relationship between songwriting and self-care that encourages students' expressiveness. "Songwriting is the core of my life and my curriculum."

Kendra's Perspective
Kendra showed us how she provided individualized instruction to meet the needs of a student, Xavier. Rather than insist that he follow group instruction, she gave him an opportunity to improvise rhythms while the group played from previously determined rhythms. "He had so much fun." Kendra concludes, "To me the biggest priority is making sure that my kids feel safe in my classroom, that they know I care about them, and I love them—even if they're not the best singer—even if they get on my nerves."

Gene's Perspective
Gene worked in a school where gang violence was prevalent. Music was an escape, a kind of sanctuary they needed. "Drumming was an outlet for their anger. They really flourished with that." He described individuals and their responses to music making: "One student was incredibly joyful, another found expression through [playing] the bass. The other thing they needed was an outlet for rap music to channel some aggression and anger. I would say aggression rather than anger." Gene commented about repositioning himself within the group. "I think [my participation] helps students feel part of the group and relate." Belonging.

Robert's Perspective
In Robert's middle school music classroom, all students are invited: "I've made it a goal to encourage all students if they have that musical itch to join the music class. There's something for everyone in this class. I'm trying to create a less exclusive, more inclusive environment." He described writing lessons to meet each child's needs: "An engaging lesson plan is not necessarily going to engage each student in the same way. A good lesson plan must be adaptable."

Marisol's Perspective
Marisol explained the importance of community building and empathy development through activities that allow students to communicate with each other, express their feelings, and talk about what's happening in the classroom. "It's really important for us to be mindful that our students know so much and that they can teach us if they are truly unafraid to tell us about something they don't like or ways we can improve." Marisol gives evidence that teachers may become learners and co-learners with their students.

Teacher-participants revealed throughout their narratives that meeting individual students' needs is complicated and demanding, especially within large music classes. Furthermore, individualization is difficult because no two students are alike—similar perhaps, but not the same. Some students need extra care to feel *safe*. Others need more guidance to feel they belong, that they are socially, musically, or intellectually compatible. Some need individual options to participate musically, such as allowing a student to improvise rhythms rather than follow note-reading, recognizing and directing a student's interest in playing a particular instrument, and offering a classroom location for a student who needs *calmness*. Children are our most valuable resource as we seek creative and confident ways to attend to individual needs—providing we let them lead the way.

Lesson plans must be flexible and adaptable; lessons are what happens in the classroom, the lived experience of children and teachers. Conversely, plans are what we intend, the decisions and preparation for short- and long-term goals, objectives, and strategies. Acknowledging the difference between lessons and plans requires new thinking about the plans we make as (1) a detailed proposal for teaching, a diagram or road map, (2) adaptable when conditions and events change, and (3) flexible when spontaneity is required.

Children Who Have Special Needs
Alice's Perspective
Alice teaches in a low-income, Title 1 school district in Brooklyn, New York, where children's needs are unmet and many children are homeless and hungry. At Christmastime, Alice organized a GoFundMe campaign for children in her school to receive presents their parents did not have resources to provide. Given its low economic status, schools like Alice's lacked basic classroom equipment, including chairs and musical instruments. To raise necessary funds, Alice learned to write a grant to buy chorus risers for her classroom, and she solicited donations of instruments, including keyboards, from local organizations and universities. There are extensive economic disparities between wealthy school districts, where children have access to instruments and state-of-the-art music technology labs, and Title I school districts, where children have inadequate equipment and supplies. Nonetheless, teachers like Alice find a way to equip their music programs.

Morgan's Perspective
Morgan is another teacher who made her students' personal needs a priority. Many of her students were poor, hungry, and without access to healthy foods. She kept a fridge in her classroom stocked with fresh fruit and vegetables. Generous and caring teachers like Morgan give their students financial and emotional support that may otherwise be unavailable to them.

Julia's Perspective
Julia contributed an anecdote about William, second-grade student who exhibited a highly developed vocabulary and extensive imagination in her music class. Julia was shocked to learn from the child's homeroom teacher that William did not read or write and spent most of the day hiding under his desk. Recognizing that William may have a learning difference, Julia initiated an evaluation that resulted in a diagnosis of ADHD. William's untreated ADHD prevented him from participating in the regular classroom; however, he was able to flourish and express himself through music. Working together, both teachers were able to meet William's needs and support him in all his classes.

Kendall's Perspective
Kendall, a seasoned music teacher and professor of music education, reported experiences working with exceptional children, many of whom were identified as being on the autism spectrum. She told us about Monty, a third grader, who was observed in a fit of pulling out clumps of his own hair. Given Kendall's experience working with special needs children, she identified Monty's neurological

condition as "sensory defensive" or sensory processing disorder (difficulties using and discriminating multisensory information). She suggested a classroom arrangement to provide a quiet corner for Monty with a bean bag chair for his comfort so that he had a place to go when he felt overwhelmed.

In a bilingual school where immigrant students did not speak English, Kendall taught the children to play instruments and communicate through music even when language was a barrier. In a different setting in rural Nebraska, Kendall met a talented piano student who had immigrated from Vietnam. The child's father had been a concert pianist who wanted a career for his son and demanded long hours of solitary practice. Despite the boy's musical accomplishment, his needs for social interaction and relationships were stronger than his father's wishes. He gave up the piano.

We teach children with special needs beyond the established spectrum of learning factors—those who suffer homelessness and hunger, discrimination and prejudice, cultural and language differences, developmental disabilities, and chronic disease. Each child who comes to our music room brings their outside life experience inside.

Consider the cogency of these questions: How much do you know about your students? Is it possible that when a child leaves your class, she heads back to a shelter, or worse yet to the street instead of a home? Could this child be living in a single room in a dilapidated shelter with seven other siblings, most of whom she takes care of herself? Is her mother struggling with addiction? Could she be sleeping on a filthy mattress on the floor while all night long mice and roaches scurry around her? Is she so terrified of being sexually assaulted in the shared shelter restroom that she and her family relieve themselves in a communal bucket? Is there hope that she and her family will ever break the endless cycle of poverty and homelessness? What would this child need from you, her teacher, that is different from what her classmates might need? If this scenario seems far-fetched, it is not. It is the real-life story of one child who survived these terrifying experiences.

Dr. Deborah K. Padgett, professor at New York University's Silver School of Social Work, is internationally known for her work concerning homelessness, mental health, and research methodology. We contacted Dr. Padgett for guidance in our inquiry about the effects of homelessness in the lives of children. She directed us to pertinent studies, most notably "Invisible Child: Girl in the Shadows: Dasani's Homeless Life" (2013), the first in a five-part series published in the *New York Times* by award-winning American journalist Andrea Elliott.[1]

Born homeless, Dasani lived with drug-addicted parents and seven younger siblings in a decrepit homeless shelter in one room overrun with vermin, insects, and mold. They slept on ripped, filthy mattresses and wore dirty clothes due to lack of access to laundry machines. Living conditions at the shelter were deplorable, unfit, and unsafe, especially for the 280 children who lived in this neglected former hospital. Most of these children, including Dasani's siblings, suffered severe medical issues and developmental delays.

By five years old, Dasani is taking care of her baby sister. Each morning before school, she attends to the baby, changes, dresses, and feeds her. Dasani wipes down the small fridge, checks if the milk is okay, tidies up the dresser drawers she shares, and gets the other children out the door and on the school bus.

Dasani enters sixth grade at McKinney's School for the Arts in Brooklyn. The principal, Miss Holmes, and Miss Hester, her English teacher, are the happiest adults she knows. When asked, "What will you be when you grow up?" she and her siblings all say, "A teacher!" Elliott writes, "For Dasani, school is not just a place to cultivate a hungry mind. It is a refuge. The right school can provide routine, nourishment, and the guiding hand of responsible adults." Dasani likes her school. She writes poetry and finds refuge in the routine and discipline in her school dance classes, unlike the chaos and shambles of her home life. At home, Dasani is a "parentified child" who, Miss Hester says, "is the kind of girl who will put the mask on everyone else [until] the oxygen runs out" (Elliott 2013, 167).

In her fifteen years at McKinney secondary school, Miss Holmes had known many distressed children, but few, she said, "have both the depth of Dasani's troubles and the height of her promise." Her teachers notice that Dasani does not wear proper clothes, never has anything to eat, and lacks school supplies. However, no one knows that she's often tardy because she's been up for hours doing chores even before her classmates awaken for the day. Yet, Dasani keeps up with her classes. A school counselor said Dasani has an "intuitive" approach to learning, "the kind that comes when rare smarts mix with extreme circumstances" (Elliott 2013, 31). Under five feet tall, wiry, and muscular, Dasani does not tolerate any slight she perceives as disrespect. She is quick to anger and ready to fight—behaviors that overpower her best self.

After public-school suspension, Dasani was offered a place at the Milton Hershey School in Pennsylvania. Founded in 1909, Hershey is a no-cost residential private school for low-income boys and girls. Within a month, Dasani was excelling at school, and she made the track team. Nevertheless, Dasani was homesick. She missed her family. When she went home for spring break, she wasn't prepared to clash with her siblings and to feel the discord between the two worlds in which she lived. "This is how we do this at Hershey," she would say about such things as making her bed, cleaning up, and correcting her siblings' grammar. "You changed. You actin' real white," her sister said. To Dasani, "acting white" or "talking white" were profanities she would not tolerate.

Months after Dasani returned to Hershey, she learned in a call from the Administration for Children's Services that her mother and stepfather's parental rights were removed and her siblings were placed, separately, in foster care. Dasani blamed herself. She thought that, had she been home, none of this would have happened to her family. She had not only abandoned her siblings but also the person who needed her most, her mother. "I left her too early. She wasn't ready for that leap" (Elliott 2013, 468).

Crushed by guilt and anger, Dasani spiraled downward at Hershey. Her successes in studies, sports, and self-control no longer mattered to her. "I'm gonna turn white at Hershey and I don't wanna be white. I wanna go home." After staff at Hershey exhausted all efforts to support Dasani, she was terminated for rage and violence.

Back in New York City, Dasani's transition was made difficult by changing foster home placements, continuing homelessness, and separation from her siblings. Dasani struggled with troublesome behavior that was further compromised by her destructive choices, including gang involvement, drinking, and promiscuity. Yet, she overcame it all and graduated high school and attended community college.[2]

Dasani's story is unique but not uncommon, as poverty and homelessness are pervasive throughout our country. Two and a half million children in the United States experience homelessness each year (Bassuk, DeCandia, Beach, and Berman 2014). Dr. Padgett told us that the typical profile of a homeless family in New York City is a mother with one or two children and no male parent present. She explained that securing placement in the shelter system is made complicated by intake and processing procedures and that life in a homeless shelter is highly supervised. There is no privacy.

A study by Mayberry, Shin, Benton, and Wise (2014) showed that shelter living is significantly disruptive to family routines and rituals. Children's school designation may change from one district to another, causing long commutes and thereby disrupting the continuity of learning. Any interruption to the family unit is detrimental: (1) Shelter life has no consistent dinnertime, bedtime, or reading rituals. (2) Administration of the shelter is highly controlled and often undermines parental authority. (3) The chaotic life of homeless children manifests itself at school through violence, psychological issues, and learning deficits.

For homeless children, school is a refuge of order, attention, and meals. More teachers are needed like Dasani's teachers at McKinney, Miss Holmes and Miss Hester. Teachers who understand the needs of homeless children, know how to educate them, and provide love, consistency, and protection, are vital to their survival.

No matter how or where, children find music that gives them a source of joy and delight, calm and comfort. Music, for Dasani and her siblings, is a source of personal identity, expression, and income. They go dancing in the subway with a boom box blasting Beyoncé's "Never Too Much." In one day, they got sixty-two dollars in tips tossed in a shopping bag. Dasani choreographs a new dance routine. They move to another busy train station and dance to Beyoncé's "Love on Top." On the way home, the sisters dance in tandem to I Am DLOW's challenge dance.

Dasani knows every word of her grandmother and mother's sacredly held song by Luther Vandross: "A House Is Not a Home." The lyrics speak about how *people* create a sense of home—not places or objects. Dasani also sings "This Girl Is on Fire" by Alicia Keys, a song about finding inner strength and never backing down. All of the children have heard "Papa Was a Rollin' Stone" so many times they know and can copy all the instrumentation in the recording. It's their mother's song of her father.

Dasani likes her dance classes at school, but it is street dancing that she excels at. At a party gathering, she breakdances to Willow Smith's "Whip My Hair"—thrashing her head from side to side, doing backflips and one-handed cartwheels, and balancing on her head while moving her feet in scissor chops.

Dasani and her siblings use popular music like a soundtrack to their daily lives. They sing and dance to family songs passed down and to the latest hits from R&B, pop, rap, and soul. In a special issue of the *Journal for Popular Music Education*, we contributed research articles that focus on the role of popular music within the family and how families are connected through music shared across generations (Sole and Cali 2022). Similarly, Dasani's story confirms music's power to strengthen and fortify the bonds that sustain her and her family.

Music therapists have studied the intervention of music programs that serve the needs of homeless children: songwriting with children (Fairchild and McFerran 2019), music experiences of homeless youth (Sample 2019), nurturing young children and families through music (Pasiali 2012), and music's effectiveness on social skills (Staum 1993).

There are few studies by music educators about the musical experiences of young children in homeless shelters. One exception is *Engagement with Young Children Experiencing Homelessness: An Exploratory Study*, conducted by Dr. Diana Dansereau (2020), assistant professor of music education at Boston University. She examined the impact of music classes on children, ages three months to three years old, who attended an early childhood learning center housed within a homeless shelter. Dr. Dansereau asked the center's classroom teachers, "incredibly skilled, committed, and dedicated," to participate in the study. Their observational reports and the researcher's documentation completed the exploratory study. Dr. Dansereau found that despite the stress, frequent illnesses, and developmental delays of the infants and toddlers she studied, "they were just as engaged with music as their non-homeless peers." Dansereau surmised that preservice teachers would greatly benefit from interacting with children in a nonhoused, homeless setting. We call for additional research and teacher preparation to address music learning for children outside mainstream educational opportunity and achievement.

In the present study, teachers revealed the day-to-day challenges of teaching and fulfilling the needs of children. Data narratives indicated extensive accounts of children who suffer homelessness and hunger, discrimination and prejudice, cultural and language differences, development delays, chronic disease, and mental disorders. Here, we endeavored to represent the lives of *all* the children we teach, those who are well cared for and economically advantaged and those caught in cascading cycles of poverty and inequality. In an autobiographical poem of resilience, rapper Tupac Shakur wrote about a rose that grew from concrete. It had learned to breathe fresh air, even "when no one else cared." Children, like the rose, never give up, nor should we give up on them.

Notes

1. Subsequently, Elliott wrote an extensive account of Dasani, her family, and the history from slavery to shelters in Brooklyn, New York: *Invisible Child: Poverty, Survival and Hope in an American City* (2021).

2. Andrea Elliott's connection with Dasani and her family lasted over ten years. In her 602-page book, she tells the life stories of Dasani's ancestors, of tragedies that befall her and her family, and the power of their resilience. Elliott explains the complex issues concerning poverty and inequality thorough extensive research, including analyses of children's services funded by government agencies.

ESSAY FOUR

Music and the Spiritual Child

> A child's spirit is like a child, you can never catch it by running after it; you must stand still, and, for love, it will soon itself come back.
>
> —Arthur Miller, *The Crucible*

"Music and the Spiritual Child" addresses the least acknowledged and less studied attributes of children. In analysis of data from our research participants, teachers shared insights on children's characteristics of kindness and goodness; however, few expressed thoughts on children's expression of spirituality. Exceptions were Alice, Cassidy, and Jordan, each of whom employed meditation, mindfulness, or yoga practices to create moments of stillness and calm with children.

When Jack's high school band visited a memorial site, he noticed a student who became emotionally distressed. She associated a composition the band played with the memorial. Jack consoled and assured her in a meaningful response, saying,

> This means you're a musician, an emotional artist who appreciates the passion beyond the form. The best part about this experience is that the feeling doesn't go away and that your desire to experience this again and again will not go away. You recognize this connection in the power of the art and the power of it to express emotions; the power of it to inspire others.

We seek to know if there are prevailing associations between children's experience of music and of spirituality. From ancient times to the present, suppositions about spirituality have been debated, attested to, and transcribed, particularly in religious texts. However, few researchers have investigated children's spirituality from the child's perspective. We assert that children's spirituality resides in the child's *knowing* beyond their conceptual resources and ability to verbalize their encounters with the extraordinary. We suggest that children's engagement with music supersedes the necessity for language to know and respond. "Music can name the unnamable and communicate the unknowable" (Bernstein 1976).

Michael Polanyi, in *The Tacit Dimension* (1966/2009), theorizes that tacit knowing cannot be articulated verbally but comprises the foundation of all knowledge. He suggests that objectivism or explicit knowledge cannot explain all things we humans hold dear and cannot prove—beauty and music, goodness and spirituality. Polanyi's most quoted phrase, "They know more than they can tell" (4) illuminates our understanding of very young children's interplay with music. Yet unnamable, music's elements and aesthetic qualities are nonetheless constant influences in children's lives of reality and imagination.

Robert Coles, Harvard professor and child psychiatrist, enunciated profound insight into children's inner lives through his extensive studies of children throughout the world. In a Pulitzer Prize–winning five-volume series, *Children of Crisis*, Dr. Coles reveals children's personal thoughts concerning matters of race, poverty, isolation, and morality. "Over the years, I've asked children to tell me who they are—by saying whatever words they wished to say or drawing whatever picture will enable them to forsake words for a visual statement" (Coles 1967, 308). Coles applies these methods in his book *The Spiritual Lives of Children* (1990). Here, he seeks to probe the meaning of the lives of Christian, Jewish, and Muslim children. Coles (1990) explains that his "effort [is] to blend poetic insight [and] unite ultimately the rational and the intuitive" (10).

In interviews of over five hundred children about their spiritual lives, Coles is careful to avoid a therapist's bias as he elicits children's responses. He found that as spiritual pilgrims or seekers, children of all cultures and faiths do their best to make sense of their being. In the following excerpts, Coles recalls what he learned about the spiritual life of children from a ten-year-old Hopi girl.

> The sky watches us and listens to us. It talks to us, and it hopes we are ready to talk back. The sky is where the God of the Anglos live, a teacher told us [God is a person]. She asked where our God lives. I said, "I don't know." I was telling the truth! Our God is the sky, and lives wherever the sky is. Our God is

the sun and moon, too; and our God is our [the Hopi] people, if we remember to stay here [on consecrated land]. This is where we're supposed to be, and if we leave, we lose God. (Coles 1990, 25)

The Hopi child continued:

Do you see birds on trees, how they leave, to get a drink or a bite to eat, fly away, and others follow, and the whole day goes by, birds and more birds? We become birds when we die. We fly away, but we come back. I know because . . . I feel myself sometimes wanting to lift off, go right to the mesa and have a feast: eat our bread, stand in a circle, and hear my grandmother talk about our people.

Children everywhere are profoundly aware of their spiritual connections to each other, their communities, and the worlds around them—even earlier in life than most adults realize. Let us begin at the beginning of prelinguistic knowing. From their first breaths, and some say before, prenatal and newborn infants are poised to respond to music. Joel Krueger (2013), in *Empathy, Enaction, and Shared Musical Experience: Evidence from Infant Cognition*, writes that infants are "active perceivers. Moreover, within these early interactions, music plays—or *can* play—a crucial role in drawing out and guiding early communicative exchanges" (177).

Sandra Trehub (2003) asserts in *Musical Predispositions in Infancy: An Update* that children do not begin life with a musical blank slate, but infants are predisposed "to attend to the melodic contour and rhythmic patterning of sound sequences, whether music or speech" (abstract).

We propose that musical knowing and sentience are prescient and communicative in infants before language emerges and before cognitive reasoning fully evolves. This means that our baby-knower is an active participant in the ongoing life process of knowing.

As we seek to understand the mysteries of human learning, we are required to acknowledge ways of perceiving an object or idea from the outside *and* from within. In any act of knowing, both these features or characteristics are inseparable, as in the mind and body's response to patterns of sounds and music, and ultimately toward human endeavors in the search of the good, the true, and the beautiful.

If we connect our adult selves with our early selves, we might better understand the musical and spiritual selves of the children we teach. As individuals, we have the potential to deepen our awareness of music and spirituality in our lives as creative, imaginative, and artistic teachers. In the following example, we demonstrate the distinction of *direct knowing* (tacit) and *knowing about* (explicit) as children respond to music unfamiliar to them.

In a music lesson, "Music Tells a Story," with seven-year-old children, I asked, "Let's listen to this song. How do you think the singer is feeling as she sings?" I (Danette Littleton) played a recording of Mirella Freni singing *Un bel di* from Puccini's *Madama Butterfly*, pausing for their responses at three sections: introduction, lyrical, and dramatic conclusion. Note that none of the children knew her story or understood the words of the aria sung in Italian. Following are individual boys' and girls' pure and unprompted responses, an instance of children's direct knowing music without knowing about it.

Part One [*One fine day...*]
"She's feeling hopeless."
"She's feeling betrayed."
"She's remembering her childhood."
"Her past is sad."
"Someone died."
"She is worried."

Part Two [*I'll wait and wait...*]
"She wants to fight back for what she did wrong."
"She feels guilty."
"She is sorry."

Part Three [*Banish your idle fears, for he will return. I know it.*]
"She gets her hope back."
"She believes in herself."
"She is ready for the future."
"She has the courage to do something."
"She is peaceful."

How did these young children know what they knew? Consider that over time, philosophers debated and theorized about music's meaning, psychologists studied music cognition, and educators applied music teaching methods and strategies; however, children's experience of music, such as reported here, is rarely addressed from a child's perspective.

Nortjé and van der Merwe (2016) proposed to study the meanings young children ascribe to their experiences of connectedness during music classes. Qualitative data revealed themes for analysis: music is the best; my body dances; music takes me places; we can play together; you and me; I feel better; you can have mine. The authors write, "Music classes in early childhood education could be useful in creating opportunities for spiritual experiences, promoting connectedness and consequently fostering children's spiritual well-being" (Nortjé and van der Merwe 2016, abstract). To explore this topic, Nortjé and van der Merwe apply Van Manen's pedagogic methodology of lifeworld existence as lived space (spatiality), lived body (corporality), lived time (temporality), and lived human relation (relationality) in *Researching Lived Experience* (1990).

Ruth Wills (2011), a music teacher of children aged five to eleven, observed a change in the behavior and well-being of children engaged in singing in the school choir. Her speculation resulted in a study of spirituality and well-being on children's signals of transcendence, connectedness, and flow, as optimal experience. Wills prepared fourteen questions for prepared themes involving six children (only five participated), selected according to criteria:

Balance of genders (three boys, three girls)
Balance of ages (nine, ten, eleven)
Balance of religions and cultures (Catholic, non-Catholic, Muslim)
Range of needs (low literacy, behavioral, attention, and self-esteem issues)

Data analysis yielded responses concerning students' experience of singing in choir. Wills reported that there appeared to be a dominant theme within each child's response, as if "signatures" (Wills 2011, 43–44).

Transcendence
"When I am at choir, I forget about everything else at school and at home. I can show my feelings and express myself" (Child 1). "It's like I can do something at last; I feel proud when I have sung, like being at the Bridgewater Hall, singing with all those children. It makes you feel special. Singing with other people is better, it gives you a feeling" (Child 4).

Flow or Optimal Experience
Intention and attention: "It's an opportunity. You can really concentrate on something and make it better, then you feel better. Singing with others makes your voice sound better. It helps you be a better singer" (Child 3).
Accomplishment: All children said that they felt good after a performance, feeling a sense of accomplishment. "I feel really good at choir and when we sing like at Christmas in the Hall. It makes me really happy. I like

it when teachers smile and tell us we have done well. It's like a feeling inside. You can feel it. It's the best thing in school" (Child 5).

In conclusion, Wills (2011) writes, "Beyond the social and enjoyable aspects of music, I believe in its power to transform" (45).

Regarding the nature of children's spirituality: Is this sensitivity, like music, universal in human consciousness? In part I, "Orientation," of his book with Rebecca Nye, *The Spirit of the Child*, David Hay (1998/2006) sets out a distinction between religion and spirituality and its theological, social, and political complexity. Throughout his explication, he reviews scholarly references that interpret spirituality. Hay cites Alister Hardy, zoologist, who first asserted the viewpoint that "spirituality is rooted in something as concrete as breathing or eating or seeing." This is to say, spirituality is biologically natural to the species *Homo sapiens*. Hay continues, "What he [Hardy] is saying is that there is a form of awareness, different from and transcending everyday awareness, which is potentially present in all human beings, and which has a positive function in enabling individuals to survive their natural environment" (Hay and Nye 1998/2006, 10). Spirituality as natural selection.

In part II, "Investigation," Rebecca Nye presents the results of a three-year investigation of children's spirituality from their own voices. She explains that to analyze their conversations, she followed a grounded theory approach. That means the data and results were obtained by line-by-line computer searches for particular words and patterns. "We wanted to see if it was possible to expose a core category that would 'tell the story' of the phenomenon being studied . . . the category which drew together all the different kinds of seemingly relevant data was a compound property which I called *relational consciousness*" (Hay and Nye 1998/2006, 113). She writes, "In this 'relational consciousness' [it] seems to lie [within] the rudimentary core of children's spirituality, out of which arises meaningful aesthetic experience, religious experience, personal and traditional responses to mystery and being, and mystical and moral insight" (Hay and Nye 1998/2006, 114). Nye provides a complete list of the categories based on the full body of research, and in the following text she provides brief narratives and analysis of selected data (Hay and Nye 1998/2006, 120). Following are two excerpts on the individuality of children's spirituality.

Ruth is a six-year-old with a lively sense of wonder and delight and an active spiritual imagination. She has attended Sunday school but commented that her experience was not a source of her spirituality. Here she describes what heaven is like:

A mist of perfume, with gold walls, and a rainbow stretched over God's throne . . . but a transparent mist, like a . . . I can't explain it. Like a smell. A real cloud of smell, a lovely smell . . . like the smell you get when you go to sleep, and you wake up on a dull winter morning, and then when you go to sleep, and you wake up, and the birds are chirping, and the last drops of snow are melting away, and the treetops simmering in the breeze, and it's a spring morning. . . . [Then she added:] I suppose it's not a season at all, not really, because [it's] just a day in delight, every day. (Hay and Nye 1998/2006, 95)

Ruth's imagination expresses her love of nature and her appreciation of the mysterious transformation of everyday life. When asked by the researcher what kind of moments might lead her to think about God, Ruth said, "When I see um . . . the trees bursting into life. In spring I like that. But when I see the lambs in Wales, oh . . . it makes me . . . oh . . . leap and jump too!" (Hay and Nye 1998/2006, 96).

Tim is ten years old. With his family, he has no religious affiliation, but he speaks of animal reincarnation, polytheism, afterlife, morality, and free will. In contrast with Ruth's outward knowledge of spirituality, Tim's responses indicate an inward spiritual struggle as he questions the meaning of God and the universe: "Which God's real? Um . . . I just can't figure it out. . . . When I'm thinking about the universe, that gets me quite annoyed sometimes because I can never think about um . . . get the right answer or even get near it and um . . . then, well . . . things . . . you just wonder" (Hay and Nye 1998/2006, 97).

Nye commented that while these two children presented quite different experiences of spirituality, neither were exceptional cases, meaning that other children were equally forthcoming and thoughtful (Hay and Nye 1998/2006, 99). Hay writes,

> The search for and discovery of meaning may directly form an aspect of developing spirituality. In childhood as a sense of identity is sought for, established, and deepened; questions are raised which are essentially spiritual: Who am I? Where do I belong? What is my purpose? To whom or what am I connected or responsible? (Hay and Nye 1998/2006, 74)

Children spoke of goodness and being good and of kindness and being kind.

Ten-year-old Louise described a "magic" kind of change, suggesting a personal transformation:

> When I was being rude to my mum and stuff I . . . I like I was a new person . . . coming out of something . . . like . . . like . . . I don't know what's wrong with

me, though I'm a new person from a flower or something. Because I'm going, "I'm a new person and I'm not going to be rude to my mum." Makes you feel really, really good actually.

Some spoke of death, not in fear but as a positive spiritual resource: "Grandma looks down on me and helps me when I'm in danger." Daniel, ten years old, reflected on the death of the grandmother he had never met but with whom he "ought" to have had a relationship as natural as with living parents and siblings. When Hay and Nye (1998/2006) speak of relationality, they direct us to the relations between child-people, child-world, and child-God through which children experience awareness of self and spirituality (125).

Our story of Yolanda, in essay 2, "The Aesthetics of Care," is no less a story of spiritual transformation. Unliked, unloved, this angry preteen child guarded her private self so no one could see and only she could know. It was a song, her private self-song, that gave her solace: "There's a hero if you look inside your heart." Despite the rift with her classmates, she agreed to face them and sing: "And you cast your fears aside and you know you can survive, so when you feel like hope is gone look inside you and be strong." Significantly, this musical metamorphosis took place in a classroom, and it was felt by singer, classmates, and teacher as in a shared experience of spirituality.

What distinguishes this musical event as spiritual? Van der Merwe and Habron (2015) offer a conceptual model of spirituality in music education derived from academic literature, specifically Van Manen's (1990) lifeworld existential themes: lived space (spatiality), lived body (corporality), lived time (temporality), and lived human relation (relationality). We recognize these lifeworld themes in our story of Yolanda's spiritual transcendence through music: in a lived space (spatiality), expressed through her voice and body (corporeality), made meaningful through personal awareness and connection with others present (relationality), and lived time (temporality).

The authors embedded personal events as vignettes of spirituality in music education as part of the interpretation of Van Manen's four themes. They suggest that this model has potential for researchers who conduct qualitative studies including grounded theory, narrative research, ethnography, phenomenology, and case study. Furthermore, they state that the model "could help describe and explain the lived experiences of learners and teachers" (Van Manen 1990, 63). They propose that their model might be used with preservice teachers to foster awareness and sensitivity of time, space, body, and relationship for spiritual well-being within the contexts of music education.

When spirituality in young children evolves into adolescence, it signifies a life journey. As teens gain more freedom in the outside world and encounter new experiences, they seek identity and place of being. Psychologist and specialist on children's spirituality Lisa Miller (2013) refers to the transition into adolescence as a spiritual awakening: "[It] surges like a tidal wave and brings with it a hunger and an ability to experience the transcendent relationship, the desire to feel a transcendent connection with other people, and a sense of being part of the universe" (67).

Adrian-Mario Gellel, in "Children and Spirituality" (2013), writes, "The difference between a young child and an adolescent's spirituality is highlighted by studies in the area of psychology and youth development" (124). He explains that as adolescents evolve from the childhood experience of spirituality, they seek to establish personal identity, connection with others, and a commitment to life purpose. Gellel introduces a relatively new area of research, positive youth development, that "takes into consideration the holistic and relational development of the adolescent." In his work, "spirituality is understood in relation to other aspects and dimensions of adolescent life in an attempt to understand how spirituality may contribute to the adolescent's well-being" (124).

Ari, a teenage boy on a pilgrimage to understand and express his private and secluded musical world, found a lifeworld transformation of time, space, body, and relationship. The following narrative presents his discovery of music, learning, and teaching, mind to mind and spirit to spirit between student and teacher (Danette Littleton).

Ari was a junior at an elite high school when I met him. The headmistress, a friend of mine, asked if I'd meet with a student who was doing poorly in his classes. "He's into music." He was polite when we met, but I could tell he would rather not participate. However, he agreed to a second meeting. I asked if he would bring recordings of music he liked. *He gave me a teen-age eyeroll that said, "You won't like it."* At the next session, he brought a huge CD folder of heavy metal groups, some I knew, but most I had never heard of. "So, tell me about this music."

In a role reversal that rarely occurs in an educational setting, I positioned myself as learner and Ari as teacher. As we studied together, our musical and analytical curiosity converged as each of us learned new repertoire. For example, we studied Lost Breed, Tantrahead, Holst, *The Planets*, Yngwie Malmsteen, *Rising Force*, Morbid Angel, Mozart *Requiem*, Mahler symphonies (first, second, third, fifth, sixth, ninth), Prokofiev, *Romeo and Juliet Ballet* (complete), Mussorgsky, *Pictures at an Exhibition* (orchestra), Alice in Chains, Berlioz *Symphony Fantastique*, Dreamtheater, Rimsky-Korsakov, *Scheherazade*, Amorphis, Ravel, *Daphnis and Chloe*, Mr. Bungle, and more.

Ari was responsible for (a) selecting the repertoire for each session; (b) providing CD recordings, if possible, or asking me to locate them; and (c) engaging in listening and analyzing musical elements, style characteristics, and performances. This strategy was designed to maximize Ari's musical interests by (a) starting with what he knows, (b) directing his attention to musical elements as a function of style, (c) revealing his musical perceptions and discussing "What do you hear?" (d) guiding his musical understanding toward interpretation, (e) establishing concepts and technical terms of musical criticism, (f) expanding his sense of "modern" and "classical" style characteristics, and (g) developing a foundation for the study of styles, traditions, and genres of Western art music, music of world cultures, and traditional and popular music.

When Ari described elements, characteristics, or functionality of a given performance, he often spoke of "virtuosity" and "intensity," and when he turned attention to instrumentation and songwriting, he identified structure, form, and composition. Given his astute discussions of metal groups, one day I asked, "So, I notice the symphony is playing Mahler Six. Wanna go?" From then, we continued to attend symphony concerts, talking together at intermission and afterward about what we'd heard. At following school sessions, I played recordings of the same work with different orchestras and conductors for his comparison and analysis. Ari's listening and analytical skills continued to develop, always original.

By graduation, Ari did well in all his courses and received high marks on his international baccalaureate exams, including music (Hay and Nye, 119–37, for examples). Ari's deep engagements with music learning; choice of repertoire; respect for his ideas, analysis, and criticism; self-awareness and confidence; personal goals; and growth contributed to a transformation that was spiritual in its manifestation.

The final report to Ari's parents and headmistress included my evaluation:

> During this evaluation period, Ari's progress has been continuous and significant. Specifically, his musical perceptions with the capacity for description and interpretation have advanced considerably. This is due, in part, to Ari's self-directed goals for increased musical knowledge, understanding, skills, and his growing confidence, overall. Examples include a) emphasis on learning musical terms, b) attention to new and challenging orchestral works, including orchestration, score reading, and memorization.

Of particular importance is Ari's decision to commit to the added demands of writing the IB [international baccalaureate] senior essay that requires, in written form, his skills of musicianship, analysis, and intellectual originality. During the preparation stage of his paper, Ari planned the outline, major ideas, artists' interviews, repertoire, relevant score excerpts, and audio tapes of selected musical examples. As his research evolved, he decided to narrow the focus of the paper from investigating Metal bands, in general, to studying aspects of soloing and virtuosity among selected electric guitarists and violinists. This is an ambitious and original topic that Ari is uniquely qualified to accomplish.

No less significant than his success in music listening, analysis, and scholarship, Ari has made important progress in related areas of musical interest. He has reorganized his band, set new directions for himself in composition, and applied for university study in music.

Ari's musical talent, creative intelligence, and commitment to personal goals assure him continued success in his musical pursuits.

Despite their differences in age and cultural and economic resources, Yolanda's and Ari's stories have common elements of learning and teaching and personal relationality. Stories of students like these are waiting to be told by music teachers in classrooms across America.

In a later essay, we pursue self-knowledge as leaders, parents, and teachers toward understanding our significant function in support of children's musical and spiritual development.

> Ubuntu is the Xhosa word used to describe the "tend and befriend" survival behavior. Ubuntu recognizes that human beings need each other for survival. A person is only a person through other persons, we say. We must care for each other in order to thrive. I am because you are.
>
> —Archbishop Desmond Tutu and Mpho Tutu (2010)

PART II

~

PEDAGOGY

ESSAY FIVE

Children's Play with Music

> For children, play is the bridge between inner life and external reality.
> —Daniel Challener (1997, 3)

The greatest asset in the child's process of learning is the impetus to play. It is through play that children first seek to understand and be understood. Studies of children's play in various settings confirm their predisposition for play and reveal individual personalities as they engage others. When a child calls out, "Let's pretend!" every other young child knows "the game is afoot!" When they answer the call, there is no prescribed agenda, plot, or theme. Soon an idea pops up and the actors, props, and scenes emerge as stories within a story.

Four-year-old Jay calls out, "Pretend this is my room." At once, Jay and Jennifer begin to construct a playhouse using the musical instruments, xylophones, and mallets to outline a space on the floor.

Jay: Come on, Jenny. We can share. This is both our bedrooms.

Jenny: We don't have more mallets. This is the hallway.

[Belinda joins the play.]

Belinda: If we move this (xylophone) and this (xylophone) . . .

Jay: You can't have this. This is my room. Pretend me and Jenny have to stay in our room, because we don't know where to go, because we are blind.

Jay [*picks up the claves*]: Pretend this is my very own toy.

Jenny: This is my instrument.

Jay: You got ALL the mallets. We can share them.

[*Belinda rearranges the xylophones to create her own room.*]

Belinda: This is my whole room. You can't go past this.

Jay: I have a BIG room.

Jenny: You can't go past.

Belinda: Quiet.

Jenny: And our house is made of instruments!

Jay: Yeah! We can make our rooms hooked together!

All yell: YEAH!

[*They begin to play the xylophones and continue simultaneously until Jenny suggests that they bring all the other instruments in the music room inside their house.*]

Jenny: What about the PIANO! Oh gosh, we can leave that!

Jenny [*shifts the story line*]: It's lightning!

[*She plays loud sounds on the lower register of the piano.*]

Jenny: Put on the roof!

Jay: Hurry! Get into our house!

Belinda: Oh no! It's raining!

[*All scramble inside the house.*]

Jenny: We are all snug and tight inside! Now we are cuddly inside!

[*They pass the instruments, previously placed inside the house, to each other, sharing and playing together. Belinda introduces a new idea.*]

Belinda: Let's do "Jingle Bells"!

[*All sing "Jingle Bells" and accompany their singing with bells, triangles, and cymbals.*]

Belinda: This looks like a house! Look, we cleaned the whole room up (the music classroom).

[*Belinda's comment interjects a moment of reality; however, the others ignore it and continue the music instruments house play theme.*]

Jenny [*rings the triangle and sings*]: Time for bedtime . . .

[*Immediately, all lie down on the floor inside the house and pretend to sleep.*]

Jenny [*plays the triangle and sings*]: Time to get up.

All: Thank goodness! Thank goodness!

Jenny [*plays the triangle and sings*]: Time for breakfast.

[*All use the small percussion instruments as pretend utensils and food.*]

Jenny [*plays the triangle and sings*]: Play . . . time.

[*Jay introduces a variation on the music house theme.*]

Jay: Pretend it was Christmas!

Belinda: And Santa Claus comes to our house FIRST! Just like he always did.

Jenny: Yeah, and we say it's midnight.

All: Lie down on the floor and pretend to sleep. [*Without any verbal clues, they jump up and yell*] HE'S HERE, HE'S HERE!

[*They continue yelling and celebrating as they "discover" the musical instruments and begin playing.*]

All [*shouting to each other*]: Look what I got! Look what I got!

Jenny: Oh, my gosh! WE GOT A WHOLE PLAYROOM!

All [*yelling and cheering*]: He brought us all the toys we wanted! We're rich! Look at what he gave me!

Belinda: Give me that violin! That's what Santa gave me.

Jenny: I got an instrument crown! [*She places a tambourine on her head.*] We got to speak French! [*She babbles in a high-pitched voice, speaking and singing in faux French.*]

Jay: Look what Santa gave me. [*He plays the autoharp.*]

Jenny: He gave us all these toys!

Jay: He gave all the toys . . . and . . . we . . . SHARE!

The music drama continues as the children play the instruments, at times rhythmic and patterned or nonmetric. They created free-flowing melodies and played fragments of nursery songs. Whether brief or extended, their explorations and improvisations appeared deliberate and independently created.

Dramatic play with music usually involves a group of children, each taking turns at directing the narrative. In the following example, Caroline demonstrates constructive play with music. Her exploration of a single instrument exhibits musical structure through discernible rhythm patterns, tempo, and dynamics.

Alone, Caroline sits down at a large Chinese gong. She takes the mallet and repetitively taps the gong and listens as the sound fades. She begins to play a pattern of eight to ten beats, slower to faster, softer to louder. She pauses and listens. Caroline plays the same musical pattern fifteen times in succession and each time she pauses and listens. Without interruption, she replays her distinctive percussion motif seven more times. Caroline's play episode continues for twenty minutes without interruption. Her exploration and invention with the gong demonstrate the four-year-old's thoughtful organization of musical elements of tempo, dynamics, and rhythm within a formalized structure.

At the next session, one week later, the children returned to the music play setting, and Caroline went immediately to the gong and reproduced her creation. It had remained in her memory, intact, over time. During several weeks of data collection, Caroline was observed frequently playing her Chinese gong music. Her improvisation yielded an emerging composition in all ways except transcribed into notation.

Another example of children's constructive play with music involves two four-year-old boys. Greg and Ken engage in a musical game of their own making with contra-bass xylophone bars. Each boy picks up one of the mallets provided, and they take turns playing each of the three bars, tuned to C, E, and G, respectively. Soon, they begin to imitate each other's playing. They look at each other and laugh at the fun they're having. The dueling xylophone episode escalates as they add leaps, jumps, and exaggerated arm movements with the mallets. Neither boy speaks. Their musical conversation speaks for them with steady beat rhythms, short melodic sequences that are created, repeated, and copied. In subsequent play episodes, Greg and Ken invited other boys and girls as willing partners in their musical game.

Jay and Ryan use three tall African drums to build a drum tower, one on top of the other. Carefully, they strike the sides of the drums with mallets, making drum-talk with their six-foot drum totem.

Functional play of young children in a free-play music setting is characterized by exploring ways of playing with musical instruments and eliciting varieties of sound-making. Functional play episodes are brief as children move from one instrument to another. In the first play session, the children enter the music room quietly. They seem awed by the amount and variety of instruments. Initially, there is little discussion or negotiation about choices. The teacher says, "Come in, children. This afternoon, the music room is prepared for you to play and make music." As children enthusiastically move about the room, their chatter increases and sounds of instruments swell.

Sara Smilansky's (1968) generative work on children's play provides an underlying structure in this study of children's play with music. Smilansky modified Jean Piaget's (1962) theory of play development; she modified and developed four categories of cognitive play:

1. Functional play, simple repetitive movements with or without objects.
2. Constructive play, manipulation of objects to create or construct something.
3. Dramatic play, imaginary situations created to satisfy the child's needs or wishes.
4. Games with rules, acceptance of prearranged rules of conduct or procedure.[1]

Numerous play researchers have followed Smilansky's categories; however, the present study was the first to apply her cognitive play categories in a free-play music setting. A second substructure in this study concerns children's social play with music. Parten's (1932) influential work defined categories of social participation:

Uninvolved: Child is active but does not engage in play.
Onlooker: Child attends to others' play but does not participate.
Solitary: Child plays alone.
Parallel: Child plays near or beside others but not with them.
Associative: Child plays with others.
Cooperative: Children share common goals of play and negotiate tasks and roles (Frost, Wortham, and Reifel 2008, 43).

Adaptation and refinement of Parten's taxonomy were applied to the present study of children's social play with music.

1. Solitary play is observed when a child pursues their own activity without reference to what others are doing.
    a. Tara's solitary sustained play with the violin, in one play session, continued for twenty minutes.
    b. Caroline's solitary first encounter with the Chinese gong continued for thirty minutes and she resumed play in the following four music play sessions.

c. Separately, Daniel, Greg, Bret, and Jay each engaged in solitary play with lengthy episodes with melodic and percussion instruments.
   d. Belinda demonstrated a preference for prolonged solitary play episodes, including singing, dancing, and playing the piano.
   e. Holly played alone for an extended event by arranging several instruments in a circle around her and creating a one-girl band performance.
2. Parallel play occurs when the child plays alone and independently but close to other children, often using similar play equipment. Children's parallel play with music shows that they imitated each other's playing in patterned and spontaneous improvisations:
   a. Meghan improvises rhythmic and melodic patterns on an alto xylophone.
   b. Nearby, Ken and Greg are playing the contra-bass xylophones. Soon they begin to imitate Meghan's improvisations. They do not speak or interact with each other.
   c. Tara places a tambourine on her head. Holly notices and finds another tambourine and places it on her head. Across the room, they dance to the jingles of the tambourines.
3. Group play occurs when the child plays with other children in a similar, identical, or supplementary activity. They engage in verbal and nonverbal communication. They borrow and loan play materials and initiate a play theme or dramatic situation. Children's social play behavior with music occurred as two or more children engaged in dramatic play themes.
   a. In extended episodes, children engage in storytelling with musical instruments, movement and gestures, vocalizations and singing.
   b. In dramatic play of family themes, children spontaneously assumed roles as babies, parents, grandmother, mother as a music teacher, and cats and dogs.
   c. Children created a dramatic play theme about a thunderstorm that caused a house fire. Scenarios were created by their use of instruments, dialogue, and role-playing.
   d. Constructive play with music instruments prompted a Disney-style theme with singing and dancing as princesses and villains.
   e. Children created unusual uses of small percussion instruments, triangles and strikers and finger cymbals, as tools in a dentist office scenario.
   f. One four-year-old girl assumed the role of music teacher. She gathered instruments in rows, placed a music stand in front, and selected

a mallet as a baton. With everything in place, she called each student by name and assigned them an instrument. She directed the playing: "You start when I point to you. When I go like this, you stop." She held authority for twenty-five minutes until another child wanted to be the music teacher. Quickly, the conductor said, "Oh, you can be my daughter."

These excerpts are from a study of four- and five-year-old children's free play with music (Littleton, 1991). This inquiry was prompted by the need to know what children's natural music making is like in a noninstructional setting:

How is music known to you?
How do you make music with your voice, body, found sounds, and musical instruments?
How do you play, explore, and create music, alone, with playmates, without instruction or adult intervention?

Presented here are real-life episodes of one group of twelve boys and girls who were offered an opportunity to enter a prepared music space for the sole purpose of playing. Results show that their music making was in all ways unique and meaningfully different from the traditional music curriculum for young children. New perspectives on children's musicality emerged from observations of children at play with music. Here, we discovered what we did not know about children's musical ideas, improvisations with instruments, spontaneous singing, moving in response to music of their own making, and interactions with others in creating music dramas. Such new knowledge, from the child's perspective, best informs our future decisions on curriculum design and instructional strategies. What we did not know previously does not mean that there was nothing to know.

Of 177 references to "play" in our transcriptions of teachers' data, there are three references to children's musical play. Primarily, teachers referred to "play" in relation to playing in an ensemble and playing an instrument. That instances of spontaneous musical play, playfulness, dramatic play, or teacher-facilitated play are missing from our data confirms the need for further investigation of children's naturalistic engagement with music. Such knowledge is essential to our understanding of young children's musical culture and our relationship with them.

Dr. Sole collected video journals from fourteen future music teachers enrolled in a graduate course, Designing Musical Experiences for Young

Children. Reviews of their journals revealed a significant interest in musical play. Main themes emerged, such as (1) concern that creativity and play have been "edited out" of student teaching in favor of dedicating class time to more "concrete measures of success" that can be assessed; (2) recognition of the value of musical play and the need to reconsider the design of teaching plans; (3) space and time for free musical exploration and play, not just as an "add on" to the end of a lesson; and (4) trust in children's innate musicality by observing their music behaviors and interests. We have confidence in these aspiring music teachers' contributions in studying and promoting the benefits of children's musical play and suggest this knowledge can help teachers, at all stages of their career, to foster openness and creativity in their classrooms.

Teachers who are parents have unique opportunities to share musical experiences with their children. They become co-players with children at home and bring that relationship to children in their classrooms.

Gene's Perspective

Gene, a teacher-participant in our study, recalled hiking with his young daughter and using natural elements in creating a woodlands orchestra. He emphasized taking great care to follow her lead as they created music together. Gene shows how parents may best participate with their children by playing according to children's inspirations and rules.

Abigail's Perspective

Abigail, another teacher-participant, described how her experiences as a mother of a young son influenced her teaching:

> Most importantly, I have had to relearn what it means to play. To really let go of any agenda or expectations and just engage my imagination—without any kind of rules or limitations on what I should or should not be pretending. I see and hear him [her son] mimicking many of my styles and moves, and voices. Also, I try to listen and watch what he does, and then adopt his ideas, which seems to encourage him to do more and not shy away.

She continued, "It allows me to model alternatives for my students and 'what if' kind of scenarios as we develop curriculum and interact with children." Abigail remarked that preservice teachers need to experience being with young children, in the moment, as they create and make music. She described facilitating an improvisatory drum circle with second-grade students. Upon reflection, Abigail said that she was astounded by the children's musicality, improvisations, and motivation to play without any guidance from herself. The lesson stayed with her and it "changed everything that I thought I knew about teaching."

Abigail added,

> As a music teacher-educator I just wish that my students would have as much time as possible being with children, playing with children, remembering what it means to PLAY!!! I am planning to create musical play groups with my students and community children for observation and play. Let children lead and explore/discover—in a space where they don't feel they need to meet standards, or learning targets, no agenda, no deadline—just see where the possibilities take them.

Laughter often erupts as children play—in fact, humor is its own type of play. In "Children's Humor," Jennifer Cunningham (2005) writes, "First, humor is enjoyable in the ways that most play is enjoyable. Second, humor constructs an unreal world—much as make-believe play does. Third, the enjoyable, unreal world of humor often performs the same cognitive, social, and emotional functions as play in general" (94). Humor, like play, is not serious. Make-believe play, silliness, incongruity, surprise games, and spontaneity do not belong to the real world, and the real-world rules do not apply.

Play is fun and children at play are right comedians, as the following vignettes demonstrate:

Jenny uses two mallets as walking canes. She play-acts as an old lady walking unsteadily, her knees wobbling, hands shaking, and her voice is high-pitched and weak.

Margaret: Who's that?

Jenny: My grandmother. Her teeth are falling out.

Margaret: Here grandmother. We'll take her to the dentist.

[*The girls use a triangle striker to look inside grandmother's mouth. They place finger cymbals and metal bars from a glockenspiel on her head.*]

Margaret: We need these for treatment.

[*Onlookers laugh at the scenario. The girls laugh, too.*]

In another episode, Jeremy picks up the Miss Piggy hand puppet. He improvises various vocalizations from high-pitched squeaking, growling, to singing, "I'm Miss Pig-----gy." As he sings, Jeremy waves the puppet through the air and runs around the room. Placing a mallet in the puppet's mouth, he plays a glissando on a xylophone and then on the piano. Nearby, Greg joins Jeremy's Miss Piggy puppet with the Kermit puppet. The boys engage in a singing game of chase, until Miss Piggy sings, "I'm a giant frog eater!" In response, Kermit sings, "Ohhhh, I wish I was in the country." The boys laugh and put down the puppets. Game over.

Later, Meaghan asks the boys, "Hey! What happened to Kermit? What happened to Miss Piggy?" Jeremy replies, "They're music lovers again."

Holly's hilarious play episode with a pair of cymbals made her playmate laugh. Holly hangs two cymbals by their straps on a drum mallet. She tips one end of the mallet and then the other end causing the cymbals to make contact and ring. She plays with them in this manner for a while. Then, she balances her self-made mallet-with-cymbals instrument on her head. Each cymbal hangs down over her ears. Belinda laughs, "Stop that, Holly! You look like a mouse!" Holly knows how funny she looks, she laughs, too.

Children and musicians, dancers, actors, writers, and other mammals engage in and love to play. They share attributes of spontaneity, curiosity, joyfulness, imagination, humor, and resiliency. In his classical study of *Homo Ludens*, man the player, Johann Huizinga (1938/1950) posited that humans in their earliest stages of civilization played and that the "play spirit" of joy, pretend, and nonseriousness has been a major civilizing force in human development. Play, in human history, is the cradle of art.

In Wennerstrand's (2021) article "The Playful Ways of the Performing Artist," she compared the similar ways performing artists and children play. "In the freest sense, play is doing for its own sake. Play is embodied behavior, and through playing with the elements he or she loves, the performing artist creates the vital essence of live performance" (442). She explains that "in dance, theater, and music, play provides the means to explore and communicate in a flexible way." Furthermore, she cites the revolution in dance singularly created by Isadora Duncan, the mother of modern dance (1877–1927). Duncan rebelled at the precision and restrictions of classical dance; in contrast, her inspiration came from nature and the natural movement of the human body. Duncan's expressive dances included elements of children's free movements at play, such as skips, jumps, walks, runs, hops, spins, and twirls. In addition, Wennerstrand shows how performing artists' embodiment of the element and spirit of play directly emanates from child's play. It may be inferred that children's play with music forecasts a lifelong musical engagement of musicians and educators.

Elliot Eisner (1990), one of the most influential scholars of the arts in education, wrote, "Both art and play like imagination and fantasy are not regarded as a part of the serious business of schooling. To be serious requires clear goals, and a well thought out plan of achieving them and, perhaps most of all, hard work. Neither play nor art is associated with work" (43). He added, "To paraphrase Aristotle, 'Play like art, loves chance.'" Eisner explains that artists and children create forms that convey aspects of their experience. "It is in these forms that meaning is embedded, and it is the cultivation of multiple forms of literacy [ways of knowing] that such meanings are recovered" (55) and that "different forms of art [and play] call upon different aspects of being" (54).

Thus far, we have addressed how children play with music and how it contributes to their cognitive, social, and musical development. We have presented relevant theories of play and art in human development. Furthermore, we have indicated that children's humor and playfulness are primary traits that are easily subdued or lost in standardized schooling.

Finally, we submit that teachers develop music play opportunities to enhance children's learning by revitalizing curriculum, creating new strategies, and redesigning music learning environments. To create opportunities that allow children to explore music's qualities, we need to know what the child knows, how they express themselves with music, and what matters most to them. To better understand, we need to invite children's reflections as they advance in musical knowledge and skills.

Vivian Paley (1991, 1993, 2009) championed the importance of listening to and observing young children at play. Fundamental to teaching, she collected and analyzed detailed notes of children's play events and storytelling events. When we observe, take notes, and record children's behaviors in different settings, we find that music play behaviors carry over in classroom activities. *How do children play with music on their own?* The reverse is also true: classroom experiences carry over to play activities. These are ways music play episodes might be incorporated into music lessons: invite children to extend their music making in the play setting to an instructional setting, for example, Caroline's Chinese gong improvisation; Greg and Ken's dueling bass xylophones; Jay and Ryan's drumming; Belinda's improvised song; and Miss Piggy and Kermit's singing conversation. A second option is to incorporate several music play episodes into a classroom lesson. Third, suggest ways children can create a picture or line drawing score of their music. Fourth, guide children in re-creating one of the dramatic play episodes as an in-class performance.

Perhaps the most important source for understanding children's play with music is our own memories of childhood. Remember how music felt to you? Did you have instruments, or did you make music with found sounds? Did you sing and dance like a rock star? Did you perform scenes from musicals or create your own music shows? Did you create backyard performances with siblings and friends? Childhood memories will revitalize your excitement, fun, and joy of playing, creating, and performing music. Modeling these qualities in your classroom will inspire the children you teach and enliven learning and teaching experiences.

Final thoughts: true play, like true art, must be pure and beautiful.

> It may be that this aesthetic factor is identical with the impulse to create orderly form, which animates in all its aspects. The words we use to denote the elements of play belong for the most part to aesthetics, terms with which we try to describe beauty: tension, poise, balance, contrast, variation, solution, resolution, etc. Play casts a spell over us; it is "enchanting," captivating." It is invested with the noblest qualities we are capable of perceiving in things: rhythm and harmony. (Huizinga 1938/1950, 10)

Play's greatest contribution to civilization may be its ability to teach humankind to respond aesthetically in a world where order and harmony are at a premium and the paradise of a nurturing childhood seems to be slipping away.

Note

1. Games with rules do not apply to this study of free play.

ESSAY SIX

Wonder-Filled Knowing and Learning

We introduce this essay with a lengthy quotation from Rachel Carson. No one captures the wonder of children as she does in *The Sense of Wonder* (1956/1998):

> A child's world is fresh and new and beautiful, full of wonder and excitement. It is our misfortune that for most of us that clear-eyed vision, that true instinct for what is beautiful and awe-inspiring, is dimmed and even lost before we reach adulthood. If I had influence with the good fairy who is supposed to preside over the christening of all children, I should ask that her gift to each child in the world be a sense of wonder so indestructible that it would last throughout life, as an unfailing antidote against the boredom and disenchantments of later years, the sterile preoccupation with things that are artificial, the alienation from the sources of our strength. (42)
>
> If a child is to keep alive his inborn sense of wonder without any such gift from the fairies, he needs the companionship of at least one adult who can share it, rediscovering with him the joy, excitement, and mystery of the world we live in. Parents often have a sense of inadequacy when confronted on the one hand with the eager, sensitive mind of a child and on the other with a world of complex physical nature, inhabited by a life so various and unfamiliar that it seems hopeless to reduce it to order and knowledge. In a mood of self-defeat, they exclaim, "How can I possibly teach my child about nature—why, I don't even know one bird from another!" (43)

> I sincerely believe that for the child, and for the parent seeking to guide him, it is not half so important to know as to feel. If facts are the seeds that later produce knowledge and wisdom, then the emotions and the impressions of the senses are the fertile soil in which the seeds must grow. The years of early childhood are the time to prepare the soil. Once the emotions have been aroused—a sense of the beautiful, the excitement of the new and the unknown, a feeling of sympathy, pity, admiration, or love—then we wish for knowledge about the object of our emotional response. Once found, it has lasting meaning. It is more important to pave the way for the child to want to know than to put him on a diet of facts he is not ready to assimilate. (45)

Wonder is little children's superpower. It is their way of knowing what is direct, instinctual, and untaught. Children in their earliest years experience the world as wonder-filled. Wonder and play are buddies. They engage children with feelings of surprise at the unexpected with accompanying expressions of fascination and delight. In nature as with music, children need no words to acknowledge or apprehend the sights and sounds they encounter; instead, they express what their bodies feel. Picture babies playing peek-a-boo and the joy of surprise in their faces and bodies along with irrepressible laughter, or toddlers hiding and gleefully waiting to be found, or preschool children doubling over with belly laughs at a start-and-stop music game. Laughter at the unexpected is sweetest in children.

Children's experience of wonder exists in the moment, engages the senses, and resides in the spirit as well as the mind. In this way, children, like all of us, are one of a kind and all the same. However, what is most important to know about children may be hidden in plain sight, waiting for us to discover and embrace. In *Nature and Selected Essays* (2003), Ralph Waldo Emerson gave us this analogy of the immediacy of wonder: "If stars should appear one night in a thousand years, how would men believe and adore; and preserve for many generations the remembrance. . . . But every night come out these envoys of beauty and light the universe with their admonishing smile." And yet, we forget to look. We stay inside and watch TV. Instead, let us wander outside, take a child's hand, and seek wonder in the stars, the stars they see.

In *Inventing Imaginary Worlds: From Childhood Play to Adult Creativity Across the Arts and Sciences* (2014), author Michele Root-Bernstein says, "This [book] is the story of worldplay." An invention of her own, she defines what she means by "worldplay":

1. The invention of an imaginary world, sometimes called a paracosm [parallel world].

2. In childhood and youth, an outcome of the normally developing imagination, often associated with play in sacred, found, and constructed places.
3. Self-generated make-believe tending to the sustained modeling of a hypothetical place or system.
4. In the arts, a plausible pretense; in the sciences and social sciences, a possible world.
5. A touchstone experience, a creative strategy. (xi)

Worldplay, presented here, significantly broadens our frame of reference regarding the concepts of wonder and play. As children, we spent hours at play, inventing imaginary worlds in a place and time of our own making. Some of us created imaginary playmates to join us. In those embryonic worlds, notable novelists, musicians, dancers, and artists have their professional origins. In *Imaginary Worlds*, Root-Bernstein (2014) describes the childhood drawings by C. S. Lewis of his imagining. In mapping and chronicling Animal-Land, he believed, "I was training myself to be a novelist" (9).

At age four or five, Wolfgang Amadeus Mozart created elaborate fantasy kingdoms in which he was king, where he could reign supreme, free of real-world restraints. His sister, Marianne, four and a half years older, played as queen. Later, Marianne wrote,

> He would think out a kingdom for himself as we traveled from one place to another. This kingdom and its inhabitants were endowed with everything that could make of them good and happy children. . . . He was King of this land . . . and he carried it so far that our servant who could draw a little, had to make a chart of it and he [Mozart] would dictate the names of the cities, market towns, and villages to him. (Solomon 1995, 66)

One can only image that his kingdom was filled with music.

Misty Copeland, the first African American woman in seventy-five years to be principal ballerina with the American Ballet Theater, recalled entering the magical world of *Coppelia* upon seeing a film of the ballet when she was seven years old. Mikhail Baryshnikov said of his early years that he rebelled against his military father to enter the world of ballet.

Artists Wassily Kandinsky, Henri Matisse, Paul Klee, Pablo Picasso, and Joan Miro spoke of the continuing influence of the freshness and imagination of their childhood drawings. In a retrospective titled *Looking at Life with the Eyes of a Child*, Matisse remarked that "the artist . . . has to look at everything as though he saw it for the first time: he has to look at life as he did when he was a child and if he loses that faculty, he cannot express himself in an original, that is, a personal way" (Fineberg 1997, 18).

A German contemporary of Matisse's, E. L. Kirchner, wrote in a diary that "the artist is after all the free responsive child, who reacts to each new stimulus, . . . not in any logical or historical sense, but reconstructing them in his dreams [or imagination]" (quoted in Fineberg 1997, 19).

Joan Miró told his biographer, Jacques Dupin, "The older I get and the more I master the medium, the more I return to my earliest experiences. I think that at the end of my life, I will recover all the forces of my childhood" (Miró and Dupin 1993, 138).

Charles Baudelaire (2018), the French poet, regarded the child "as having a raw receptivity to the 'correspondences' between the visible world and higher truths that underline it, a clairvoyance like that of the poet or artist but lacking in the analytic skills to fashion this intuition into art. The child sees everything in a state of newness" (5). Baudelaire recognizes children's receptivity to the visual world and their *clear vision* of an artist; however, unlike Kandinsky, Matisse, Klee, Pablo Picasso, and Joan Miró, he dismisses children's drawings as art because they lack analytic (and technical) skills. Such emphasis on adult measures of children's art is restrictive and for some children discouraging.

Mendelowitz, in *Children Are Artists* (1953) wrote, "A child's paintings, drawings, and sculptures are some of the many ways by which he expresses his reactions to his living experiences" (18). Children's artistic expression through drawing, inventing stories, and making music first emerges in their play and reveals to us the child's ways of thinking and envisioning their worldplay domain. In essay 5, "Children's Play with Music," we demonstrated that spontaneous and imaginative play affords individuals and groups of children opportunities to create original music. The anecdotal records reveal children's keen interest and ability as musicians, without instruction.

By what means do we reconcile the distinction between taught and untaught aspects of music in the education of children? Consider the prescribed or semifixed curriculum as a symbolic structure rather than a strict formation—like clouds of knowing and learning where children's imagination and wondering and the acquisition of musical knowledge and skills are not separate. Alfred North Whitehead (1929/1963) said it best: "You may not divide the seamless coat of learning." We suggest that *being in* music with awe and wonder cannot be separated from the alignment of taught and untaught components of learning and teaching.

In *Inventing Imaginary Worlds*, Root-Bernstein (2014) commented on observations by educational philosopher Maxine Greene: "When others limit the child's choice of action, imaginative or otherwise, the kind of self formed may very well be a conforming self" (184). Greene believed that children use what they have been taught, take in new learning, and without instruction seek new knowledge—as in "wondering about."

The private and unobserved world of children as they engage in make-believe play is in all ways unique to the individual child. For some children, early experiences are formative to adult lives as writers, dancers, musicians, and painters. For children, these often-solitary involvements captivate their inside-outside lives of feelings and imaginings. Seminal childhood experiences such as these last a lifetime, and when remembered they awaken our selfhood.

When we involve ourselves in the visual arts, music, drama, and literature, we enter artistic and aesthetic realms of separate realities—our own worldplay—that mirrors children's imagining and creating worlds of wonder. The music room, like no other classroom, can be the place where teacher and children live together and share feelings and emotions summoned by musical experience.

We were surprised that while a few teacher-participants in our study referenced a "wonder-like" characteristic of childhood, only one recounted a wonder-filled experience from her childhood. It was Cassidy who told us about a special memory of music when she was in elementary school when the music teacher turned off the classroom lights and, as she played recorded music, she gave each child a scarf and invited them to lie down, listen to the music, and follow its flow with their scarves. Cassidy recalled feeling that as a group, they "melted away" into the music. "We shared a powerful aesthetic experience." Cassidy noted that transcendent experiences in her music class seemed to disappear around third grade, when skill acquisition became the focal point of music learning.

We are called to present a musical repertoire worthy of children's sensitivities. Composer Zoltan Kodály famously said that only the best music should be reserved for children. *What to you is the best music?* For a moment, recall music that is most meaningful to you—from childhood to the present, of differing styles and genres. Perhaps it is the music that you performed as a soloist, or in a choral or instrumental ensemble, perhaps a concert you attended. As you choose music that serves your goals and students' interests, be mindful of music that inspires you. Your students will be inspired; and in turn, they will inspire your teaching. Choose teaching strategies that allow for what may be called a "curriculum-of-the-moment" when children's wonder-filled responses and ideas might take new and unexpected turns. Improvise. *It's all jazz.*

Worldplay, as symbolic structure, offers ways of musical world making inside the music classroom with a group of children under the umbrella of pedagogy. In this open setting, unlike children's private settings, teachers may prompt, guide, or direct activities in creating musical worlds with children.

For example, you may choose music-world themes such as contemporary realms of space and time; historic events of time, place, and culture; and fantasy kingdoms: "Music in the Time of George Washington." "Music Long Ago and Far Away." "Music of the First Peoples." "Music in the Land of Magic." Remember C. S. Lewis as a child mapped and chronicled a literary world, and little Mozart created a magical kingdom unique to his fantasy world. Think about children—like you were back then and children you know now—absorbed in imaginary world making. Know that knowledge, imagination, and make-believe are innate in each child's growth and development and that they thrive and flourish through living engagement with their world.

Professor and scholar Dwayne Huebner (1999), in the article "The Capacity for Wonder and Education," proposed, "They [children] share their world with their teachers, they are not equals of their teachers, for they are of greater worth; less conditioned and freer. Potentially, they can give more to the world than the teacher for they have more energy and fewer fixed and uncreative ways" (32).

Huebner's comments may seem upside down until you compare children's magical thinking with our own more structured thinking. We were schooled in compartmentalized curricula by means of separate disciplines and sequential hierarchies of difficulty. By comparison, young children, not yet schooled in curricular subjects or taught names of things, are "free-range" thinkers, awe-struck explorers of uncharted territories. Music, to them, is all things connected to learning and making. Theirs is an age of discovery, of music, fine arts, dance, of drama and stories, a generative era of world making and wonder.

This essay seeks a new way of thinking about the children we teach, their identity, interests, what they know, and how they learn. Given this perspective, we have a one-of-a-kind opportunity to bring together children's wonder-filled knowing and learning through musical knowledge, understanding, skills, and passion for teaching.

> The pursuit of truth and beauty is a sphere of activity in which we are permitted to remain children all our lives.
>
> —Albert Einstein

PART III

PROMISES

ESSAY SEVEN

Knowing Those Who Teach

> Every childhood has its talismans that look innocuous to the outside world, but that trigger an onslaught of vivid memories when the grown child confronts them.
>
> —Steven Johnson (2010)

These are difficult times for music teachers, and yet those in our study and countless others persist. There exists in their hearts and minds a desire to make music that enhances the children's lives and their own. The decision to teach music is affected by our passion for music and by the influential relationships and personal factors that motivated us to share it.

The teacher-participants in our research study told of their experiences with the children they teach, including reflections of their own childhood experiences. Many shared personal stories of family members and music teachers who made long-lasting impressions on their lives. Some shared stories about the absence of adult support, when as children they found music as a source of comfort and belonging. As you read the stories of our teacher-participants, you may ask, "What is *my* story, and what led me to answer the call to teach music?"

External Forces: Environment and Musical Mentors

In his book *The Courage to Teach: Exploring the Inner Landscape of a Teacher's Life,* author, educator, and activist Parker Palmer (2017) emphasized the importance of mentorship in a teacher's life. He writes about the power of a mentor to model great teaching and passion for a particular subject, to "awaken a truth within us" (22). He links mentorship to mutuality, a condition where the best qualities of both mentor and student are revealed in a relationship characterized by true intimacy.

The Promise of Mentorship
Many teacher-participants were influenced by great mentors from their childhoods. Some spoke about their family lineage of music teachers. Bennett's father and Shane's mother were accomplished band directors. Shane noted the impact of his music teaching legacy, telling us that he's been "a band kid my whole life." Shane studied jazz performance and only recently began to study general music education. He spoke of "learning to teach through teaching itself" and about emulating his late mother. Bennett's high school choir director and his father, a music teacher, led Bennett to teach music.

The Promise of Family
According to our teacher-participants, family support and influence are key motivators. Kendall and Geoffrey spoke about the positive encouragement they received from family members who guided them toward becoming music teachers. Kendall told us about family members who were accomplished, professional performers. Geoffrey talked about inspiration from his supportive mom. Morgan said her strict parents dissuaded her pursuit of a musical career and said they would withhold financial support for college if she decided to become a teacher. Determined, she found encouragement from an orchestra teacher and her uncle, who was a musician.

The Promise of Musical Mentorship: Support and Understanding
Many participants were inspired by their childhood music teachers. Bob credited his high school band director, who helped him realize his passion for teaching during his time in school and after graduation when Jack invited Bob to coach the marching band drumline. They formed a lasting musical connection as colleagues and friends.

From teacher-participants, we learned how musical mentors provided support and encouragement. Some participants described themselves as shy, introverted children who found confidence and self-expression facilitated by caring musical mentors. Geoffrey's music teacher instilled a love of piano and confidence to explore and question. She was a "mentor who made us believe in ourselves and in the collective group." Melody was barely four years old and desperate to play piano. Only one teacher took a chance and accepted her into the piano studio, thus helping her realize a childhood dream of making and teaching music.

The Promise of Mentorship: Safety and Acceptance

Musical mentors provided a sense of security and acceptance for children like Walter, shy and introverted. Not until playing in the school jazz band did he feel a sense of belonging. His music teacher gave him good advice and friendship. "I think that music was a place where more students, including myself, could feel a sense of being at home, feeling a place within a larger community."

As a gay man growing up in South Carolina, Robert credits a mentor who inspired him to accept himself even before he was ready to come out. "I was embraced and given the right material that was age appropriate to really help me." Jack's music teacher cultivated a safe environment, free of judgment or ridicule, where he was able to experiment and explore.

The Promise of Mentorship: Wonder and Purpose

Childhood mentors cultivated an environment characterized by creativity, joy, and wonderment. Gene recalled his "amazing mentor" who valued improvisation and creativity and led him to value a childhood of wonder and innocence where teachers encourage autonomy, trust, and respect. Similarly, Cassidy recalled her mentor, whose teaching captured a sense of "joyful wonder."

Musical experiences and relationships in childhood were significant for those who became music teachers. At the beginning of her teaching career, Katie revealed, "My purpose is to teach, to make sure that these kids know that there's at least one space where they know that they're loved and that music is something that should bring joy to them, not discomfort or fear." As an experienced music teacher, Jack shared his calling to teach music: "Being a music teacher is such a part of who I am that I can't imagine life without it. I can't imagine not being what I am. I think, ultimately, this is what I was destined to be: a music teacher."

The Absence of Mentorship: Finding Oneself in Music

Examples of musical mentorship illustrate positive ways that family members and teachers support and encourage children to pursue music. When mentors are not present, children persist to find solace, comfort, and identity in music. In essay 4, we met Dasani, a child born into homelessness, who moved around to numerous shelters with her seven siblings and drug-addicted parents. For Dasani, there was no mentorship or support system. She and her siblings turned to music as a source of expression and a passage toward personal identities.

Internal factors and unnamable life forces motivate teachers in their choice of profession. David Hansen, in *The Call to Teach* (1995), refers to an inner power or calling, fulfilling and meaningful, that shapes and expresses personality identity. In a later book, *Reimagining the Call to Teach* (2021), Hansen explored teaching as a soulful commitment through lived experiences of joy and suffering.

In "The Art of Teaching," Dwayne Huebner (1999) writes,

> When we regard teaching as vocation, acknowledging that it is a way of living and not a way of making a living, and if we attend to the meanings and value making of the teacher, we will rebuild our educational communities so that we live more truthfully, justly, openly, and beautifully in the classroom. (387)

Huebner considered teaching as art. He believed that teachers face complexities as complex as life itself—situations filled with doubts, conflicts, and humor, as well as bleakness and beauty, pathos and love, anger and laughter, all complicated by unpredictability and adjustment. Nevertheless, teachers-as-artists synthesize all these parts into a wholeness that brings children to a heightened awareness of meaning and possibility.

A Passion and Love of Music

Robert Grudin (1990), American writer and philosopher, wrote, "The fundamental motive of true teaching is the love that seeks and studies and performs. True teachers not only impart knowledge and method but awaken a love of learning by virtue of their own reflected love" (147). Teacher-participants, speaking about their passion for teaching and performing, used the word "love" ninety-eight times in the data transcripts. Trevor said that teaching music is an act of "sharing your joy and passion." Jack referred to himself as an emotional artist who understands the passion within the art form. He noted that students can tell when a teacher has a true passion for music. Grace said, "As music teachers we love music, and we love expressing ourselves through it." Geoffrey said he was driven by a desire to discover ways to connect and respond to his students.

The Soul of the Teacher

Parker Palmer (2017) asks us to consider the spiritual element in the hearts and souls of teachers. Good teaching "holds a mirror to the soul," and if teachers are willing to see that reflection, they will truly know themselves, their subject, and their students. "Are we doing enough to help teachers in training understand their inner terrain in ways that will minimize the shadow and maximize the light?" (378). He proposes a "pedagogy of the soul" that engages art, poetry, and music to realize our voices as teachers.

Parents and clergy may be spiritual mentors to children as are teachers. In our essay on spirituality, we focused on children as spiritual beings. Here, we consider how teachers call on their spirituality to support children's experience. In "Teaching and Religious Imagination," Maria Harris (1991) casts a new light on teaching. She writes, "Teaching, when seen as an activity of religious imagination, is the incarnation of subject matter in ways that lead to the revelation of subject matter" (xv). Teaching music is a journey of spiritual imagination and wonder, "to name the unnamable" and "address the non-ordinary" (16). Harris suggests that allowing ourselves to connect with the intangible aspects of teaching reveals "a capacity to be suffused by wonder and surprised by joy in an instant" (61). Huebner (1999) supported Harris, writing, "Every mode of knowing is a mode of being open and venerable, and available to the internal and external world" (349).

We, the authors, offer recollections of the meaning of music in our early lives:

Danette's Vignette
My earliest childhood memories of music begin at three to four years old. Typical of young children, my musical memories are not limited to hearing. For me, a flood of senses accompanies remembered music like a soundtrack accompanies film images. I remember songs and sounds, sight and images, warmth, and touch when my grandmother sang to me. "In the Sweet By and By" was a song that everybody in my family sang—front porch singing, housework singing, kids singing, and Sunday morning singing. After supper, when the dishes were done and the kids cleaned up, we sat on the front porch and gently swung back and forth in the dewy twilight. Grandmama, Mama, Aunt Ruth, and Aunt Mable talked a bit of news about the neighborhood happenings. They called it wash-day news—neighborhood news mostly shared over backyard clotheslines. "Did you hear? Mrs. Thompson's having another baby." There was talk of who lost a job or needed help, of tending the sick, carrying homemade meals to the down-and-

out or taking in little children until their mamas could cope. I would be just about lulled to sleep from all their talking when Grandmama would begin to sing.

Soon, everyone joined her, including me. Songs I learned from Grandmama I sang to my young daughter. Even now on a quiet warm summer evening, old melodies wash over me in waves of comfort—"Shall we gather at the river, where bright angels' feet have trod"—of solace—"I am a poor wayfaring stranger, traveling through this world of woe, yet there is no sickness, toil or danger, in that bright world to which I go, I am going there to see my mother"—and "joy"—"I've just come from the fountain."

As I recalled memories shared here, deeply held feelings and images surfaced as in a dream. It was twilight, the light was soft and the air cool after a hot summer day. My mother and aunts were sitting there on the front porch. Grandmother and I rocked slowly in the swing, my head resting on her lap as she sang and stroked my hair. I felt that her singing was just for me. It was an unspoken bond that lasted her lifetime and mine (Littleton 2022).

Meryl's Vignette
At the age of eight, I began playing the French horn. I wanted to play the saxophone, yet my parents were insistent that the horn was a more unique and suitable choice for me. Undoubtedly, the reason for this was rooted in the fact that both my father and older sister played the horn. This musical family bond through the horn brought my father and me together while at the same time it drove a wedge between us, of joy and frustration, anger and love. While practice sessions at home usually ended with arguments and shouting, there was also a truly special connection forged between my father and me in our shared love for classical music and our love for each other.

At the age of fourteen, I began playing with a selective youth symphony in New York City. I can still picture the concert, sitting onstage at Carnegie Hall in the fourth horn seat. Low horn was my forte; you could feel the low pedal tones in your bones! There were over one hundred musicians on stage, vocal soloists at the front of the orchestra with a full choir seated on risers, directly behind the brass and percussion sections. Toward the end of the fourth and final movement of the symphony, it hit me. The chorus stood from their seats and began to sing in German, "*Seid umschlungen, Millionen. Diesen Kuß der ganzen Welt! Brüder! Über'm Sternenzelt Muß ein lieber Vater wohnen.*" I recall having a powerful feeling of both playing and simultaneously being surrounded by sound, completely enveloped. I remember the feeling in my body, the sound both inside and outside. As the "Ode to Joy" concluded, the feeling of magic and joy overtook me as tears streamed down my face. As I looked to my left and right, I saw many other fellow musicians weeping. At that moment, I wasn't aware of the translation: "You millions, I embrace you. This kiss is for all the world! Brothers, above the starry canopy. There must dwell a loving Father. Do you fall in worship, you millions? World, do you know your Creator? Seek Him in the heavens! Above the stars must He dwell." Yet, I felt a deeper connection to something bigger, a transcendent moment of connection to those around me and beyond.

Relationships foster moments of magic and expressions of love when the ordinary becomes extraordinary. Ellen Dissanayake (2000) reminds us that "the feelings of transcendental oneness that can arise while making or experiencing the arts or in religious and other poetic or spiritual transfigurations are at least in part based on these innate propensities for mutuality" (49).

As we listened to the voices of the teacher-participants in our study, we heard messages of goodness, kindness, playfulness, wonder, and spirituality. Theirs are the ethics, values, and behaviors worthy of emulating as we consider the future of music learning and teaching.

Goodness
The music teacher-participants:

- look for the root of behaviors and seek to understand each child's experience and perspective
- focus on seeing the good in every child
- view classroom management as a skill for understanding each child, not as punishment
- seek to understand behavior based on developmental knowledge
- celebrate and enjoy childlike wonder and joy

Kindness
The music teacher-participants:

- show kindness to their students, and support them beyond teaching
- model empathy, compassion, and patience, see it returned from their students
- give praise and show appreciation
- separate the negative behavior from the identity of the child
- forgive and seek forgiveness from students when wrong
- show honesty and humility

Needs
The music teacher-participants:

- redirect disruption
- individualize activities based on a child's need for expression, understanding
- use drumming and physical activity as an emotional outlet
- use humor to connect
- offer food and caring
- seek funding through grants and local organizations
- create safe spaces where students feel accepted
- encourage songwriting and composing
- adapt teaching, as necessary, to support virtual learning
- seek guidance for students with special challenges
- connect as parents care for their students

Spirituality and Wonder
The music teacher-participants:

- know themselves, and are forthright, as appropriate, about their background
- observe moments when music is transcendental
- recognize ways music connects people of different cultures and traditions
- practice and teach mindfulness and meditation
- breathe together
- connect music with real-life experiences
- cultivate experiences that engage students emotionally

Musicality and Musical Play
The music teacher-participants:

- understand children's musicality and abilities
- devote time and space for improvisation and free play with instruments
- value students' interest to explore, improvise, and create music
- celebrate musical achievements, especially those with learning differences
- emphasize musical expression
- adjust lesson plans in the moment

- follow the children when exploring and playing music together
- value students' musical self-expression and self-teaching outside the classroom

> I have come to believe that a great teacher is a great artist and that there are as few as there are any other great artists. Teaching might even be the greatest of the arts since the medium is the human mind and spirit.
>
> —John Steinbeck

ESSAY EIGHT

Toward a Pedagogy of Hope

In this final essay, we bring forward the themes of this book with a vision toward the future. In essays 1–6, we asserted the innate goodness of children and conveyed the importance of caring and attending to their needs. In seeking to understand children's spirituality, our hearts were opened to the innocence of hopefulness and trust. As we encountered children's worlds of play and wonder, our childhood imaginations were rekindled. We submit that in all ways, what we have learned about children is analogous to what we have learned about teaching.

The structure of learning and teaching supersedes decisions about subject matter, what to teach and when. In *The Aims of Education*, Alfred North Whitehead (1929/1963), distinguished mathematician and philosopher, outlined a cyclical process across the curriculum with universal application, designated "the rhythm of education" (26–32). Here, he suggests that life is essentially cyclic, such as daily periods of work and play, activity and sleep, and the passing seasons, and that "mental growth" and learning similarly pass from cycle to cycle (28). He proposes a threefold schema: romance, precision, and generalization.

The learning cycle begins with romance, that blush of delight—be it in nature, at home, at school, or wherever one encounters the magical or mysterious. It is the excitement, novelty, and vividness of apprehension that leads to the desire to know and engage. Sometimes a glimpse of the unexpected opens a threshold to something we and the children are about to learn. We respond and exclaim our emotions in voluntary phrases, while little ones express their excitement involuntarily with vocal and body languages.

As we seek to know more and as children acquire greater experience, we enter the learning cycle of precision. It is then that the learner acquires basic elements of knowledge and its concepts, and the ability to use the languages of symbols and gesture. As children discover dimensions of pulse and rhythm, melodic direction and contour, dynamic ranges, and patterns of repetition and contrast, they grow in understanding and refine their musical skills of listening, singing, moving in response to music, playing instruments, improvising, composing, and using symbolic representation and notation.

According to Whitehead (1929/1963), the third cycle, generalization, refers to a comprehensive level of attainment from the previous cycles of romance and precision. Generalization develops over time, as experience and knowledge grows.

What follows will be surprising to those who advocate stage theories of learning and teaching. Whitehead (1929/1963) makes clear that education must follow a continual repetition of the cyclical process. That is, with each new educational encounter, the learner experiences the allure of newness with enthusiasm, commitment, and devotion as the cycle continues. In contrast, methodology that promotes a process of readiness, ranking, and stage learning places prescribed objectives over instinctive and individual ways of learning and teaching. Schooling absent of affect renders learning barren and inert. Our classrooms may be the only oasis of play, wonder, spirituality, and care, where children find means of expression and individuality through music.

"What can we do now in order to be able to do tomorrow what we are unable to do today?" (Freire 1992). Previous efforts to reform public education by national mandates included A Nation at Risk (1980–1989), Standards Based Educational Model (1990–2000), No Child Left Behind (2001–2015), and Every Student Success Act (2016–2021). With each commission, states and local school districts were expected to comply. However, on such a massive scale and designed by a top-down strategy, results have been disappointing and expensive.

Conversely, symposia for music education focused on philosophical thought and promoted innovative teaching practices. The Contemporary Music Project was funded by the Ford Foundation in 1957 ($1,380,000) and administered by the Music Educators National Conference.[1] The first of these projects, the Young Composers Project, introduced by Norman Dello Joio, composer and chair, placed composers-in-residence in public schools to emphasize and assist in teaching contemporary music. From 1963 to 1973, the grant provided for establishment of seminars and workshops at universities and six in-school pilot programs in major cities.

In 1967, a gathering of distinguished musicians, educators, sociologists, and representatives of industry and government participated in the Tanglewood Symposium, "Music in American Society." Speakers included Erich Leinsdorf, "Music in a Changing World"; Sarah Caldwell and Harry S. Broudy, "The Case for Aesthetic Education"; Norman Dello Joio, Abraham H. Maslow, and F. S. C. Northrop, "The Theoretic and Aesthetic Components in the Western World"; Gunther Schuller and Ralph W. Tyler, "The Role of Music in Our Philosophy of Education"; and others (Choate 1968). The Music Educators National Conference concludes with the following declaration:

> We believe that education must have as major goals the art of living, the building of personal identity, and nurturing creativity. Since the study of music can contribute much to these ends, we now call for music to be placed in the core of the school curriculum.
>
> The arts afford a continuity with the aesthetic tradition in man's history. Music and other fine arts, largely nonverbal in nature, reach close to the social, psychological, and physiological roots of man and his search for identity and self-realization.
>
> Educators must accept the responsibility for developing opportunities that meet man's individual needs and the needs of a society plagued by the consequences of changing values, alienation, hostility between generations, racial and international tensions, and the challenges of a new leisure. (Choate 1968, 139)

The Tanglewood Declaration goals are as thought-provoking and appropriate to music education issues and circumstances today as when they were asserted fifty-four years ago. We recommend that the speeches and discussions in the *Documentary Report* are worthy of continued attention, intensive study, and reflection. In addition, we recommend studying the 1981 report *Ann Arbor Symposium: Application of Psychology to the Teaching and Learning of Music*, sponsored by the Music Educators National Conference, the University of Michigan School of Music, and a grant from the Theodore Presser Foundation of Philadelphia. Over four days, selected music educators and psychologists presented papers, as follows:

- Marilyn P. Zimmerman, "Child Development and Music Education"
- W. Jay Dowling, "Mental Structures through Which Music Is Perceived"
- Lyle Davidson, Patricia McKernon, and Howard Gardner, "The Acquisition of Song: A Developmental Approach"

- William Kessen, "Encounters: The American Child's Meeting with Music"

Other papers and responses are included in the final report.

The Housewright Symposium convened at the Florida State University, September 23–26, 1999. The following year *Vision 2020: The Housewright Symposium on the Future Education* (2020), edited by Clifford K. Madsen, was published by the National Association for Music Education. In "MENC: From Tanglewood to the Present," Michael L. Mark (2020) explains the importance of knowing our past: "The reason for reviewing past events, for studying history, is to understand why things are as they are now and to help approach the future in as educated a manner as possible" (5). We offer these documents to stimulate interest, encourage study, and inspire new ideas—*standing on the shoulders of giants* who shaped our profession, a profession defined by common purpose, shared vision, and norms and boundaries.

Throughout these essays, we center attention on the lives of children, their qualities of goodness, sense of wonder, curiosity, play, spirituality, and receptivity to beauty and joy. If we let them, they can inspire the same in us. We submit that knowledge of the child belongs at the center of music learning and teaching. While direction as to what children should learn and at what grade level is routinely prescribed, attention to mind (thoughts, feelings, attitudes, values) and behavior (social interactions, sense of belonging, coping skills) remains unattended. American schools reflect American society in all ways of problems and promises. The children we teach face increasing challenges to their everyday lives, especially those affected by poverty, cultural and racial discrimination, and social and learning difficulties. Even children whose lives are privileged by affluence, travel, and accelerated learning experiences are subjected to America's societal conflicts and global tragedies.

Teacher-participants in our study reported that the most dynamic challenge in teaching is not knowing how to care for and understand children's individuality as learners. However, in their classrooms, they showed remarkable resilience as they learned to "swim" uncharted waters by creating music experiences and environments to meet the needs of all students.

> Jordan: It's something I learned over the years. I got better at it. I was kind of thrown in headfirst and had to sink or swim.

> Alice: I feel that a lot I learned in college about teaching meant absolutely nothing throughout my teaching career—if I'm being very honest. I don't feel that I was prepared, I felt unprepared.

Nate: I wish I had learned more about the language you use to interact with children of various ages.

Bennett: Too much focus on becoming a band director, not enough on understanding children.

Trevor: A course that I thought was great was in child development, from early childhood through adolescence. It was important to me as an educator to understand why kids behave the way they do, the psychology and reason behind the behavior.

Bob: Courses in psychology and development were useful to me in understanding children.

Kendall: I'm not saying that I wished my graduate courses gave me a curriculum to teach. I'm glad I found my own identity with what I teach. I created my own curriculum, but I found it interesting how much the [undergraduate] teacher preparation program lacked.

Robert: I learned never underestimate children and be careful to witness their natural musical instincts.

Melody: I learned the value of creating detailed lesson plans.

Morgan: My whole philosophy is a student-centered, democratic classroom environment. It's a lot easier said than done. Just saying that I have a student-run classroom and having students create norms and dictate where your curriculum goes and how you get there is a scary thing, like a scary cliff to jump off. But that's been the most valuable lesson I've ever learned, so I let my students run my entire classroom, essentially from start to finish. I find I get a lot more done the more autonomy students have. At the start of the year, students make their own rules.

Notable philosopher of music education Bennett Reimer (2009), in *Seeking the Significance of Music Education: Essays and Reflections*, projected an agenda central to the improvement of music education according to

- breadth of musical studies;
- adding a composition program to performance and general music;
- broadening the philosophical and critical understanding of music educators;
- moving from methods to curriculum;
- managing the status quo of field experience; and
- teachers as researchers. (247)

As Reimer advised, these eight issues are not exhaustive; rather they are intended to address the kinds of issues about which "we need to talk, write, and reach better clarity" (247).

We submit the following improvements:

- Restructure undergraduate music education programs that better reflect a changing educational community.
- Convert disparate subjects of study into interdisciplinary courses of learning.
- Devote attention to cognitive-psychological and social-psychological dimensions of music learning and teaching.
- Seek and implement innovative curricula that focus on children at the center of learning and teaching.
- Involve music educators in planning and policy decisions with administrators at their school, district, and national organizations.
- Encourage communication and collaboration among music educators through websites and blogs.

Music teachers are optimistic and hopeful. They are dedicated to their work. Often, they are the last teacher to leave the building and the one who conducts extra-school rehearsals and performances. Music teachers keep up their performance skills; attend seminars, workshops, and conferences; and seek advanced degrees. From personal funds, they purchase teaching materials and even provide sustenance for children who need help, and if undersupplied, they find outside funding to purchase instruments and learning labs.

Children sense that their music teacher loves teaching: "Do music teachers ever frown?" Children know they are loved and valued. Upon hearing their music teacher was leaving, children cried out, "You can't leave us. You're our only hope!" Even in difficult times, we create classrooms of learning together with joy, imagination, and compassion. When we are discouraged, we draw on experiences making music with children to sustain our joy and nurture hope. The editors of Rethinking Schools (2022) declared that "joy is not a synonym for happy. Joy originates in resistance, joy is discovered in making a way out of no way, joy is uncovered when you know how to love yourself and others."

Love is the source—joy and hope are its offsprings. "A pedagogical relationship with children . . . is always founded on hope," said Van Manen (2016, 211) in *The Tact of Teaching: The Meaning of Pedagogical Thoughtfulness*. Hannah Arendt (1961) challenges, "Education is the point at which we decide whether we love the world enough to assume responsibility for it and by the same token save it from ruin which, except for renewal, except for the coming of the new and young, would be inevitable" (196).

All said, children believe in us. We have promises to keep.

Note

1. The Music Educators National Conference was renamed the National Association for Music Education (2011).

Postlude

Compassion, Empathy, and Kindness

In closing, we reiterate themes of *compassion*, the response to the suffering of others that motivates a desire to help; of *empathy*, the capacity to understand or feel what another being is experiencing; and *kindness*, a behavior marked by ethical characteristics and a concern for others that encourages reciprocity.

Getty Images. © Estersinhache fotografía.

The Kindest Survived

In [his book] *Descent*, Darwin argued that the social instincts—instincts toward sympathy, play, belonging in groups, caring for off-spring, reciprocity, acts of generosity, and worrying about the regard of others—are part of human nature. (Keltner 2009, 53)

Our moral capacities are rooted in sympathy. (Darwin 1871)

Kindness Is Controversial

1. Ancient philosophers argued: naturally kind or selfish?
2. Christian Fathers questioned: intrinsic origins or bestowed by God?
3. Renaissance intellectuals debated: social fellowship versus self-oriented life.
4. Enlightenment debates exploded: Thomas Hobbes, in *Leviathan*, avowed egoistic individualism.
5. David Hume issued a sharp rebuttal in *Treatise of Human Nature*, compared the transmission of feelings between people to the symbiosis of vibrating violin strings.
6. It was Jean-Jacques Rousseau who captured the ideas of Hume, Adam Smith, and others and turned them into a psychology of kindness of unparalleled influence in *Emile*.
7. Sigmund Freud's psychological accounting for kindness included his theories of the pleasure principle, which was all about sex.
8. Modern Western society values self-sufficiency and autonomy. Needing others signals weakness.
9. Competition in modern society divides people, winners/losers, us/them.

Postlude — 87

Somehow Kindness Survives

Getty Images. © Ghislain & Marie David de Lossy.

The Children We Teach Hold the Key to a Better World

- We are the child watchers, professional observers of children. Ours is the special responsibility to see each child as that child needs to be seen through the transparent lens of compassion.
- Children come to school with hurt feelings. They want comfort. Children come to school from homes that are chaotic and violent. They yearn for patient understanding. For some children, their emotional lives go unnoticed until a teacher pays attention.
- Compassionate teaching begins with awareness of children's lives. Awareness leads toward a pedagogy of compassion. Pedagogy, applied, invites interests in research. Auto-ethnology and narrative methodologies offer ways to seek understanding of children's hearts and minds. In this era of standardization, excessive testing, and data-driven curricula, caring for children's sensibilities has never been more urgent.

Getty Images. © FatCamera.

Always Listen to Children

And if you hear me, tell me that you hear, Lest I grow weary and forget to sing.

The heart in wonder, like a lonely wren.

—Robert Nathan (1935)

Appendix

Companion Website

Please join our community at www.knowingthechildrenweteach.com to participate in discussion forums and share your perspectives and experiences. You will also find resources and blogs.

The following tables represent data coded by category according to teacher-participants.

I. Perspectives

Theme	Select Quote(s)
Goodness	"I would say that when any student was disruptive, there was always a reason for it. It wasn't that they were 'bad'; sometimes it was really more that they had been sitting all day and they really needed to move their body, or maybe other teachers had been telling them that they needed to stop doing something when they really wanted to. They were just showing that they were engaged. One thing that I would often do with the students, if I felt they were going to be disruptive, I would start to give them some other activities to do. Even if it was just passing out rhythm sticks. Then, the students saw themselves in leadership positions and they quickly began to take any sort of disruption and bring it to a constructive manner to find joy." (Cassidy)

(continued)

Theme	Select Quote(s)
Innocence, Curiosity, and Wonder	The nature of childhood is based on curiosity, inquisitiveness, and "childlike wonder." (Cassidy)
	"Teaching music connects us with our sense of wonder and joy and innocence, like a child. I've been trying to come back to that. . . . For me, I want to retain the childlike thing about music, and I say childlike in a sense of the wonder, innocence, the creativity, and the uninhibited toughness of it all. I'm a very inhibited guy." (Gene)
Development	"I always say that students make the transition from teenagers to young adults throughout their high school careers and hopefully they're not only growing physically but they're growing emotionally and they're growing in their ability to appreciate the art form. . . . You can't tell teenagers to do anything. What you can do is tell them why they should want to do it, and then hopefully guide them and help them make that choice themselves." (Joe)
Individuality	Alice spoke repeatedly on the nature of children as individuals and not lesser than adults: "Children are humans."
	Geoffrey talks about realizing that children are not "vessels to fill up with knowledge"; they are rather innately musical and full of ability ready to be tapped into. He talks about resisting labels and categories with children, highlighting individuality.
Caring Relationships	"I wish somebody told me that when you become a teacher, you are becoming family to these kids. You are a role model, you are an inspiration, and you have a platform that can play a huge key in their lives, if you choose to. At first, I wanted to save every single child. In the first few years I cried a lot, and then I realized saving one kid was enough, so I wish somebody would have told me that." (Alice)
	"One of the things I really disliked in teaching was if I messed up or if I said something was going to go a certain way, and then it didn't because I forgot or because a fire drill happened; a myriad of things happen in the in schools, and that emotionally, was a really tough one, for me, I did not like disappointing students." (Grace)
	Kayla spoke about giving kind feedback to a student: "I wanted her to know that I saw how much she was growing. One time after she was having a particularly rough day and feeling frustrated, I pulled her aside after class and said, 'Hey, I see you. I can tell how much you're working, I can tell them what you're practicing. The assignments that you've been submitting are getting better and better. You're really doing well in class.' I essentially told her that 'I won't give up on you. You are on the right track and

Theme	Select Quote(s)
Caring Relationships	everything's going well.' That's the kind of conversation I have with students fairly often. There's a lot of self-confidence building that we do in instrumental music classes, and so this was not out of the ordinary for me to have a conversation like this with a student. A couple months later, as the student was leaving to go to high school at the end of the year and everybody's feeling a little bit nostalgic, she wrote me a note and said, 'I'll never forget what you said to me that one day, and it really meant a lot. It felt really important to be seen, like that, and I really appreciate all of your guidance.'" (Kayla)
Surpassing Teacher Duties	Alice talked about grant writing to supply her classroom with instruments and resources, organizing a Christmas gift drive for children, and providing emotional support for children who did not have any resources in her poor school. Morgan spoke about supplying food and fresh fruit for students who lacked food: "I keep fruit in my fridge for the students who do not have enough food or access to good fruit or organic fruit." (Morgan)
Care and Respect	"You want to be childlike, not childish, with your students. That always resonated with me. But when I was in schools, I often saw music teachers, and even other people, colleagues that I worked with, talking at the children or talking down to them and treating them childishly and putting lots of rewards and punishments in place." (Cassidy) "One piece of advice that was given to me in college and through different textbooks and teaching manuals that I read, was giving an option for a way to use classroom management and monitor behavior in the classroom. A lot of those pieces of advice or things that I learned ended up not being as effective as talking to my students as human beings and meeting them where they're at." (Kayla) Morgan spoke of giving each student a voice: "Now that my students have created their own rules, we all vote, and it has to be a unanimous vote on each separate rule. So that means every single student has had a say in each separate rule." "Let's treat each other with kindness and compassion and then see what comes of that. Let's just be our best selves, the best versions of ourselves, and if we're having a bad day let's communicate that so we all know." "No students are going to look at you and say no, I have no compassion for you after you've shown me compassion this whole year. As long as I give them the respect, they'll just always give it back and vice versa." (Morgan)

(continued)

Theme	Select Quote(s)
Teaching/ Modeling	"I learned in school that teaching people is far more important than the subject matter that you teach, and you can't do one without the other. You have to remember that 95 percent of the facts and details and minutiae that students learn in school are forgotten and not utilized. But learning how to be good people, learning how to be good citizens, learning how to socialize, how to express their emotions in a positive way, learning how to be members of a community; all of those things are things that they will take with them. You are trying to teach them how to be good people, how to be active learners, how to inspire them to think critically and to use their experiences in school towards all the aspects of their lives. The subject matter that you teach is merely a vehicle through which those young people grow. Empathy, kindness, and understanding is what makes it possible for them to say, 'Okay, this is an individual who cares about me as a person and is invested in me, and then is also going to teach me stuff.'" "Okay, maybe that youngster has not had an opportunity to experience true empathy or develop those neural connections to wait a minute. I don't have to always get what I want at the time that I want it. They develop things like life skills." (Joe) Jordan spoke of a "disruptive" student who found self-expression and acceptance from peers through a musical activity where students interpreted emotions through music: "He was able to accurately choose the music of his peers and what they were feeling. The students in the class were like, 'Wow, he's he really got it,' and he was able to describe the music and why he thought of an emotion. He was able to shine in that kind of environment. That was an extra special year. Designing this activity, I was able to create a space for this child to show his intuitive self and to show his peers that he's really in tune with himself and others rather than always being seen as the disrupter." (Jordan) "Blame is not something we need to be throwing around. Blame is unnecessary, especially when it comes to a classroom. I really think there's a story and a reasoning, for every action and reaction, and I think it's just important to unpack it; especially having social workers around or counselors around for those conversations as well." "Give students the benefit of the doubt and give yourself the benefit of the doubt." (Morgan) Shane spoke about mentors of kindness: "My mom passed away about seven years ago. She's the one that I try to really emulate. Her kindness, the way she did things every day, because she could do things without raising her voice." (Shane)

Theme	Select Quote(s)
Behavior	Jack spoke about addressing disruptive behaviors: "Finding out the source of these issues, why these are the issues that are happening or manifesting in those kinds of behaviors; we tend to address much more the behavior itself." (Jack)
	"I've seen a lot of different types of behaviors in the classroom. There are always at least one or two students I find who present some kind of disruptive behavior. Most of the time they're usually well intentioned, and they don't mean to be disruptive, it's just their personalities taking hold." (Nate)
Understanding	"A couple stories from the inner-city school that I first taught in as a very young teacher; I had a couple of real problems that were really fun to try to figure out. I had one child who would come in and lie on his stomach; he was in the second grade. It was my first year teaching there, and he would get on his stomach and he would beat his hands and his feet and scream the whole time he was in music class. Nothing would work to calm him; nothing would reach him; he was absolute total disruption. I had to teach around all of those temper tantrums. Finally, I ended up checking with other teachers and finding out he didn't appear to have similar problems anywhere else. I asked the old school psychologist to come in and observe and she observed the same behavior and was very traumatized by it. With further exploration, we found out that his father told him that music was for 'sissies' and that was his way of showing that he was not a sissy. So, we finally were able to get that to talk with him about his behavior in music and that did a 180. He became one of my very best students." (Julia)
	"Listening to everyone's voice and giving everyone a space in evaluating expression and creativity." (Gene)
	Morgan talks about empowering students to come up with their own community rules and solutions to problems: "I just have to be patient with it and with them. Getting it worked out on their own means we get so much more time for productivity, for working on actual instruments and performances and notation and all these other things that we need to get done." (Morgan)
Children's Needs	Alice shared her experience teaching in a low-income school where many families are homeless, hungry, and living in poverty: "Where people live, and where they come from really plays a huge role in their education and it doesn't matter how great the teacher is. It's very sad because if that stuff is not being reinforced at home, there's no way it can become a full practice in a child's life." (Alice)
	Morgan shared her experiences teaching in a low-income school where students were often homeless and hungry.

(continued)

Theme	Select Quote(s)
Caring Relationships	Bob described working in a low-income, high-needs school as well as in a program for previously incarcerated youth. He also talked about being approached by the police after a concert regarding a student who may have committed a crime.
Challenges	Abigail shared an anecdote of a student with anger: "He found musical ways to channel emotion. He stayed with me through senior year. He was really successful both in choir but also in musicals. He just did great! He was a joy." (Abigail)
	"As their music teacher, I had the space and the platform to inspire these kids to become better humans, and I did that, through music. We did lots of percussion because the kids were angry, so it actually made them feel better to hit something. Lots of singing; and a lot of singing that they liked. I realized that if I used to build my lesson block based on what my kids liked, that was actually a really great experience . . . and still is." (Alice)
	Gene described teaching in a school where gang violence was prevalent: "So the drumming was kind of a sanctuary to them. Drumming as an outlet for anger. They really flourished in that, so I think there's a lot of underlying anger with most of those kids. One of them was incredibly joyful and was looking to express themself through the bass. The other thing was that they needed was the outlet of rap music to kind of channel some aggression and anger." (Gene)
	"My first few encounters with 'Sam,' he was full of joy and excitement for music. Always willing to participate in our activities and facilitate with classmates and friends when necessary. With that, when the first marking period came around, I was confident in awarding him a four out of four. 'Sam's' classroom teacher approached me after viewing the grades and questioned my decision. I defended myself, explaining that I assessed solely on my students' abilities to reach musical objectives. That same day, after being questioned by this classroom teacher, 'Sam' had been the most disruptive and angry student I had encountered thus far. He would scream and yell, throw rhythm sticks and other materials, and do just about anything to be off task. Since then, 'Sam' has been a disruptive and distracting student; unwilling to participate, or even sit in the circle with his peers for music. Of course, I am undoubtedly questioning my abilities as a teacher and facilitator to each student's learning needs. I hope that in the coming weeks I can understand what change occurred." (Melody)

Theme	Select Quote(s)
Challenges	"There were lots of angry moments in the public charter school. I will admit I wasn't a great teacher. I didn't know how to deal with it; a very different background from students and all of them came in angry. I became angry and we would be angry with each other and there were these terrible moments of me calling home and them getting in trouble with their parents. I could feel that power dynamic in the moment. I won, but it wasn't a good feeling and I could just see the anger on the kid's face and they'd be crying on the phone; their parents are yelling at them and it's just a really bad situation. I know better, now, I didn't know better then." (Maya)
	On meeting the needs of a student, "KK": "'KK' is always feeling a wide range of emotions, but on very extreme ends of the spectrum. So, if he's angry, you will know he's angry and it will be a shouting match that I can hear from downstairs three stories down. If he's excited, he is skipping and showing excitement physically in every form and way he possibly can. I know immediately; maybe let's assign KK his own piano in class today, so he doesn't have to do that group work assignment." (Morgan)
	"One student that comes to mind, for me, is a student that I had for both general music and band. This student was generally disruptive but always in a fun, comedic way, a lighthearted sort of positive way. They always wanted to joke around and have fun, which always sounds fantastic at first as a teacher, but it can be difficult to deal with when it comes time to actually get work done. In band this student was progressing more slowly than his peers and part of that was because they were being disruptive. But it was kind of difficult to reprimand them because we were having so much fun and the other students enjoyed it and it made our lessons more enjoyable. At times, this student had to be told to stop talking, stop joking around, sit down, we need to get work done. But, to be honest, I would rather have a disruptive student who is having fun than a disruptive student who is being rude or disrespectful to either myself or their peers." (Tom)
	Bob described working with students who experience domestic violence in their homes.
Belonging	"Students are really allowing themselves to be vulnerable with themselves and their peers; expressing their thoughts and feelings about themselves and the world through music. Often this is through singing and it has been incredibly powerful." (Abigail)
	"If I reposition myself among the group, I think, from experience, that helps other students to feel like they're also part of the group, and then they can relate." (Gene)

(continued)

Theme	Select Quote(s)
Belonging	Through an anecdote about a student, Nicholas, who was shy and disorganized: "It was more about finding ways to support him. Trying finding ways to make things easier for him, trying ways to ease that transition and accepting that that was a part of who Nicholas was, but that was not going to define his overall experience in the program. By senior year he was becoming conversational and feeling comfortable in the program. I really believe the program itself allowed him to come out of his shell as a musician but also as a young man, and as a young person."
	On the band program as a place for belonging: "Band is a place for those who did not have a place in school where they feel they can express themselves. They may not have a place where they were accepted for who they are, and what they were doing."
	"Having sympathy, understanding and getting to know each student breeds understanding and the ability to meet each child's needs."
	Jack's motto for his band program: "This is what we do, and this is why we do it, and this is why it is meaningful to us. We'd love for you to be part of that." (Jack)
	Marisol talked about issues with a student, "Jeremy": "In a discussion with him in class, I used it as an opportunity to educate rather than to discipline. It was truly magical because he was able to find his voice, he found confidence within himself and I even asked to lead the song and do solos. It was just a remarkable moment. . . . I need to make sure that we're implementing community building and empathy development in the classroom. . . . So my concern was making sure that he ["Jeremy"] always felt included and welcome. Sometimes he doesn't choose to share but he's listening and he's making sure that he's making connections with the students. As time went on, and we had these activities with community building, empathy building, he became more open. The last time that he was in rehearsal is where it kind of all turned around and started to make sense for me so he started to feel like he was valued and heard, to the point that he was the one who was giving examples and actually sharing with the class." (Marisol)
	Morgan goes beyond teaching music to foster a community of acceptance and belonging by advising the school Gender Sexuality Alliance Club.
	"I've made it a goal to encourage any and all students that have that musical itch in them, to join the music class because there's going to be something for everyone in this class. I'm trying to create a less exclusive and more inclusive environment within the music classroom at my middle school." (Robert)

Theme	Select Quote(s)
Belonging	Robert relates his own childhood experiences to children's needs: "As a young child I was super controlled and nervous and I'd never wanted to rock the boat, I always wanted to fit in. I was in the South and I grew up in a religious family, and I was a closeted gay child and really just didn't want to stick out too much, which is funny because I also wanted to be a performer and wanted to create art and have an opinion be known in a public way in that way." (Robert)
Listening	On the power of observing and listening to children: "I learned how to listen to them too, and to watch them and open my own observation skills to find out what they need socially and musically so that information would guide my pedagogy and curriculum." (Abigail)
	"It's really important for us as teachers to be mindful that these students know so much and that they can teach us so much. They are unafraid, truly; they're unafraid to tell us when something is not how they like it, or ways that we can improve." (Marisol)
Relationships	"It's just like connecting with a human being, having conversations with students about what music they're into, what's important to them; connecting and understanding their goals, not just participation in the music program but in school and in life. This is something that I never was taught to consider when I was in school. It was about the students in your ensemble and how they're a contributing cog in the overall machine that is the ensemble. Student as participant to the overall thing, but not student as individual. The thing that became invaluable to me was actually just being able to connect with my students as humans who had their own preferences. It sounds so obvious now, when I say it out loud but it's something that I found really, really invaluable. It has connected with me and stayed with me all these years. Starting with the human first and then working out that way and, hopefully, that is how I would love to interact with people." (Bennett)
	"What impresses me the most is how much children love music and love people who love music, and appreciate us sharing the music with them. I was very worried when I first started teaching virtually that I would not be able to connect with my children. I actually feel a closer connection with my virtual children by looking one on one in their faces on the screen than I do, sometimes, with my life. It's a very special relationship and they're always telling me thank you and they love me." (Julia)
	On lack of relationships in teacher training: "I really wish they would have talked about relationship building and how important that is and how to do it and how to connect with your students." (Maya)

(continued)

Theme	Select Quote(s)
Relationships	"There is a student in my class right now, a second grader who's always asking for my help during the exploratory parts of the lesson. But I can tell, he also is just really enjoying my company and the chance to spend time with a big person. Seeing things like that, it makes me wish that I could provide that same kind or degree of attention to all the students in the room. There's just so many. It's hard to try to build such a strong relationship with every student. When children give me an unsolicited hug or some kind of affirmation, I guess, I always feel like I'm doing something right." "I think you should make every attempt to get to know a child, though sometimes there are so many in the music classroom for me that it is really difficult. Knowing names, I think, is so important and may take a long time, but taking every opportunity you can outside of the classroom to interact with them is a great step." (Nate) "Classroom logistics and relationship management. I've never thought of it in those terms. I've never thought of classroom management as managing kids, managing small humans." "It goes back to the idea of relationships. Relationship building, classroom logistics, relationship management. I'm just developing those relationships!" "Some will say, 'What about developing relationships with the kids, I'll just get shot down.' What it came from for me is through all these gigs and these trips, I developed relationships with a lot of those students and still talk to them." "Thinking about how you can develop those life skills in a music environment that the students can then take on with them into real life, whether they're going to be a teacher or a musician or anything else." (Shane) Morgan on responding to students as a form of "classroom management": "I learned through teaching children to just be a human. When you're actually with students, don't treat them as subordinates and don't treat them as less than they are." (Morgan) "I've had a second-grade child who has impulse-control issues as well as defiance issues. One of the things that I've been doing with him successfully this year is in the mornings; I greet him at his car for parent drop-off and spent time with him walking to class and just having a conversation that's unrelated to music and seeing how his day's going and just having an interaction with him to build some rapport. In the classroom he usually avoids work as much as possible, so if he prefers to draw, I've allowed him to have a paper on his desk with supplies to color while he listens. That has actually worked out well. He's still able to participate in discussions and has a full understanding, even though he has been coloring the whole time. . . . So that has been

Theme	Select Quote(s)
Relationships	working very successfully, and I think one of the key parts is just finding the time to build a relationship with him and making sure that he knows that you're there for his best interests, and he has a little bit of option and responsibility, at the same time."
	"Something I wish I learned in college was taking the time to get to know students better and to really spend time being personable with each student. We spend so much time talking about our content area and delivering our musical knowledge to children, but I think it's more important to build a relationship with children, before you start to deliver that content. If kids want to share, they need to have that time to just take thirty seconds to share their story for the day, something that they've got on their mind, so that they can move on to learning. It doesn't mean you necessarily need to deal with it at the moment, but you need to acknowledge that they're feeling something and then get them back into a place where they can become learners." (Tara)
Respect	"Young people and students appreciate when teachers show their frailty and humility. I think the expertise as a teacher comes in being able to help kids with things, being able to help students, being able to explain things, being able to empathize and being able to say, 'Yeah, I have problems with this; I have problems with various things and I understand where you're coming from.' . . . Let me show you, let me show you how I can help you with that particular issue. I don't think it's very often that students really want virtuosic teachers who are displaying great musicianship in the kind of obvious flashy sense." (Gene)
Special Needs	Julia shared about "William," a child with ADHD: "William was able to develop a vocabulary and all of his literary skills, even though his ADHD kept him from being able to express it in the regular classroom. I think, had we, had I not seen his brilliance in music as both a singer and someone who could do all the works and the songs but who could tell me these fantastic stories, we would not have known that he needed that intervention." (Julia)
	Kendall described an experience with "Monty," a child with autism who was having disruptive reactions in elementary music class. Through observation she was able to also determine he was sensory defensive and therefore reworked the classroom setup to work for him. Kendall also described working in schools for children with autism and severe medical issues (including terminal illness), making an effort to help children have typical experiences and interactions with each other.
Parenting	"I recognize that this is hard, I recognize that high school is difficult, I recognize that it's challenging. I recognize that it's challenging raising a teenager in this day and age, and you know we're in this together, we're partners in this together, and I'm investing and trying to make sure of that for your daughter or son." (Jack)

(continued)

Theme	Select Quote(s)
Parenting	"Becoming a parent helped me to be a better teacher. I'm certainly not saying that for everyone, there are good and bad teachers and parents on both sides of the spectrum. I think for me it's being a parent and learning about them, learning about kids through my kids. What made it even more interesting and one area I've kind of veered off to lately is both my both of my kids have learning disabilities. One is autistic and one has dyslexia and ADHD. Working with them and raising them and loving on them has really helped me to better understand what these kids who fit their neuro-atypical profile might need." (Shane)
Emotions	On teaching songwriting to express emotions: "Students eat lunch with me and we work on it every single day. I have three sessions a day with students; unbelievable. I'm a singer-songwriter, so that's like tapping into something for me that was one of the most healing and grounding things in my life. When I feel really awful, I can share my song and that's how I feel. It's like I'm getting into the game. It's something that is lifting them up."
	"So that's social emotional learning; how do we listen? However we respond, there's so much in there and the songwriting is really like a core of my life and my curriculum." (Jordan)
	"Teaching social emotional learning has become a lot more prevalent and important over the past few years and it's something that was really only lightly touched upon when I was in college. Once you're in a classroom it becomes very important to be aware of children's emotions and how they're feeling and how that can affect the way that they learn. That's something that we didn't really talk about much when I was in college." (Trevor)
	"Teaching music is a vehicle through which we explore our emotions and express our feelings." (Jack)
Individualized Learning	On working with a child, Xavier: "Instead of being like, you're not doing the right thing, you're not following the directions, you're not writing down your rhythms using the notes I gave you, I gave him sort of a different task. Every time that the group comes up to play their rhythms, you're going to create your own beat in the background, so that they will pop. And he got so into it, which is really good, because I can tell normally music class like he's not really into it much, but he was having so much fun today." (Kendall)
	Morgan provides students with new experiences like traveling to New York City and going to a musical performance for the first time: "All the students from the GSA [Gender and Sexuality Alliance Club] felt so at home and they were so comfortable. It's like the first time I saw them come out of their shells." (Morgan)
	"An engaged lesson plan is not necessarily going to engage students and each student in the same way. And a good lesson plan has to be easily adaptable." (Robert)

Theme	Select Quote(s)
Individualized Learning	"I've learned that teaching the whole child is significantly more important than whatever subject you're teaching." (Trevor)
Safety	"To me the biggest priority is making sure that my kids feel safe in my classroom and that they know that I care about them and that I love them and that even if they're not the best singer, even if they get on my nerves."
	"We're not teaching soldier musicians or teaching children and 'children will be children.' The most important thing is to make sure that they know that they are safe where they are and that they are loved and they can know that by being taught music and by having and by being challenged in music." (Kendra)
	"This is an opportunity for the students to communicate with each other, their feelings about what's happening and really connect with one another and develop the environment and culture of the classroom making sure that they understand it. Some feel safe, that they could talk about themselves, and maybe get ideas and help from their peers." (Marisol)

II. Pedagogy

Theme	Select Quote(s)
Creativity	"It was the first time I ever did an improv drum circle with first and second graders with auxiliary percussion and I just remember thinking that this was absolutely remarkable. I was terrified to do it, but then after that changed; everything I thought I knew about teaching. Their creativity and their ability to play with the instruments and the way they explored them without any instruction. They were so quickly able to create interesting musical patterns, obviously, which we later called ostinato. They could make music, in a way, beyond anything that we could have read in notation and like I said just changed everything that I thought I knew about teaching music." (Abigail)
Remarkable Moments	"Just about everybody had worked their way into their head voice and we're singing the song, I mean I was literally just crying with these little second graders who had such a struggling time of matching pitch, they did this beautifully." (Grace)
	"We finally found his singing voice, and he was able to match pitch. I remember that he was so excited. There were high fives and 'way to go' from the entire class and it was just a very joyous experience for all of them." (Tara)
Developmental Differences	"Addison came into kindergarten; she had been born totally deaf and had double cochlear implants when she was three. She had to acquire all of her speech and language, from the time she was three until the time she entered kindergarten at five, so she didn't have exposure to speech and language but she had significant exposure to music because her parents were very interested in remediating her and making sure that she had a lot of different auditory input. I was very curious as to how she would perceive music. I had never taught a child that had double cochlear implants and never had any 'normal hearing.' She responded beautifully; she sang on pitch. She liked instruments. I will never forget the day that we were doing Orff instruments, and I also got out the tone resonator bells (an old-school instrument nowadays). I started playing the tone resonator bells and her face just lit up; she said it was the most beautiful thing she had ever heard, I guess the purity of the tone and the simplicity of the overtones." (Julia)
Musical Independence	"It is really cool to watch. An opportunity where I can kind of step back and let the students take control of their own learning experience and decide how they're going to interpret and use expressive elements to perform their piece of music." (Kayla)

Theme	Select Quote(s)
Musicality	"This three-year-old boy, 'Josh,' has always been excited for music since my first lesson with his class. Always running to give me a high five, to show me his homemade drumsticks, or to sing me 'Shoo Fly,' his favorite tune right now. I have come to appreciate how music is the natural opening for creativity, discovery, and exploration in a child's world." (Melody)
Responsive Teaching	"We were doing some kind of singing game of baking things and she had come up with some cool variation on it, and she was just so happy and it was such a nice class. They're cooperative and could really go with the flow. And so, I was able to veer from my lesson plan and go with her idea. Moments like that are really joyous for me because I like to see them thinking and then taking control of their music and creativity." (Maya)
	"I don't want to waste time telling them what we're about to do when I can just do it with them because they're fully capable of doing it without so much direction." (Robert)
Sharing	"Really, I think that's important when enjoying an instrument to its fullest; the competency feels really good, which is something I try to instill in my students." (Morgan)
Diversity	"I'm playing with this idea of culturally responsive vocal pedagogy so that we could honor the vocal production that stems from students' musical cultures and the musical cultures of children; whether that is just their at-home musical cultures or playground cultures. What does that mean for how they use their voices? I'm also thinking about how students from other ethnic or racial cultures bring different kinds of vocal production and use of their voices in their singing. Most of the time in school music we spend trying to teach that out of them and teach them away from those sounds, but I believe that there are ways to teach children through the voices that they bring to our classrooms without having to teach them away from it, or out of it, I think that we can teach them healthy singing." (Abigail)
Co-players	Gene spoke about co-playing with his daughter: "Whatever her motivations for walking through the woods, she picks up this big stick and starts banging a tree and keeps a steady beat. She isn't afraid; she picked that up from school this year. She goes, 'Dad, I'll play steady beat on the tree with a stick, and you can do something jazzy.' . . . So we were listening to each other and had a little moment, and then she decided we're going to have this woodland orchestra. So, she's got the steady beat thing on the tree. I've done some beatboxing. Then we're out for our next walk in the woods, now we tend to go most Sundays for a walk in the woods." (Gene)

(continued)

Theme	Select Quote(s)
Wonder-Filled Music	Bennett shared traditional music experiences of his childhood that left him feeling unfulfilled: "It was about playing with the method book and not playing music that resonated with me. It was about being forced to practice every day. It's all the things that everyone knows about; the kind of lessons why people drop out. I valued the space to play and explore; play guitar and write songs." (Bennett)
	"Our teacher used to put music on and we would sit down with scarves where we lie still on the floor, and she would put the lights out, and play music. We closed our eyes and would just melt away. Sometimes we would listen to a piece of classical music, sometimes it would be something like a jazz piece. . . . It was total space for like an aesthetic experience, and I remember it so clearly, and I remember how those experiences stopped in third grade; we had a recorder, and we were learning to read music and, of course, this was because we were starting to get funneled into going into a band or chorus setting. I sorely missed it and then." (Cassidy)
Graduate Students' Thoughts on Musical Play	"Play is serious and essential to very young children. Designing a musical experience for a group of children, so that everyone gets something out of it—and no one is left out is incredibly challenging. A lot of my creativity has been edited out of my teaching practice in favor of more concrete measures of success. For example, a kid being able to play in tune has become more important than my kids having a good time making music or creating with each other or even just having a good time." (Krista)
	Rhett talked about leaving space in the middle school classroom for play and exploration as a central activity, not a tag-on: "I really think that play is the totality of development as children explore and gain more knowledge of the world and the music that they're dealing with. It leads to more critical thinking, better musical ability and just overall builds listening, playing, and creative habits that are conducive to the kind of skills we want to build as music teachers." (Rhett)
	Andy spoke about trusting children to learn through play: "I feel that teachers are quick to give students and children associations for things that they can usually come up with on their own. And usually, the things that the children come up with are way more fantastical than we could ever imagine, especially in a field like music." (Andy)

Theme	Select Quote(s)
Graduate Students' Thoughts on Musical Play	"It doesn't feel like we're teaching the kids how to be musical, it's kind of like we're just further facilitating their musicality and that's pretty evident through the free-play explorations." (Andy) "Children experience the world through play, and so, if we can tap into that as teachers, we are accessing a world where they can learn through play and have a really fulfilling and enriching learning experience that will be memorable for them." (Gina)
Mindfulness	"I started practicing mindfulness for myself and for my kids. I needed clarity and I needed stillness to understand where these children were coming from. They were living lives that I will never live." (Alice)
Spiritual Practices	Jordan spoke about practicing mindfulness with students: "I guess I've just always been a yogi and read spiritual books. I became certified in mindfulness based on stress reduction techniques. . . . I think it's something that our children should be learning and I also think that music education is just the perfect place to put it, if they're not going to have a separate subject in school about meditation and mindfulness. . . . We did one today and we talked about how to listen and how to respond and how to be an audience member. That's all-in mindfulness; what are the things we can say, what questions we can ask, how we listen." (Jordan) Alice has written "a motivational book for ages ten and up which teaches kids about becoming the best versions of themselves and learning it through tools and practices such as journaling and meditation." "We would sometimes stop and meditate or sometimes do movement. I would take scarves out and we put on a piece of music (and these were teenagers). This specific group that I'm talking about, we would do that, to the point where they would come in and they would be able to tell me what they needed, and they would come in and say, 'Miss B, here's how we're feeling today. Could we please take a few minutes and meditate; we need to move, because we need to clear this or that.' . . . Those are some of my favorite memories with them where we just got to move our bodies. For them to advocate and take agency over themselves when they need it." (Cassidy) Jordan regularly incorporates her love and passion for yoga, meditation, and mindfulness into her classes.

(continued)

Theme	Select Quote(s)
Spiritual Experiences	Jack shared an experience with a student, "Katie," forging a "connection between the composition, something that they had played with emotions they had experienced and then seeing it in front of them." Visiting the memorial site on which a composition was based, Katie became very emotional: "She couldn't explain it in words, but she always felt that each time she played the song, it told a story. She said she just felt like the emotions were just pouring out of her. I remember saying to her, 'Katie, you know, that means you're one of us, that means you're a musician, that means you're an emotional artist who appreciates the passion behind the form. . . . The best part about this experience is that the feeling doesn't go away and that your desire to experience this again and again will not go away and you recognize this connection in the power of the art and the power of it to express emotions and the power of it to inspire in others." (Jack) Bennett spoke of temporality and joy in the moment: "I really want them to be present in that moment and find joy in that moment, because I understand how fleeting those moments can be. Maybe they will never get to play Carnegie Hall again, or maybe they'll play it all the time, who knows? But, having the hindsight of experience and age, you want your students to really focus and be in the present moment and appreciate what they have. Those are all unforgettable experiences." (Bennett) Geoffrey spoke of spontaneous moments of flow and connection where things evolve organically in teaching and performing.

III. Promises

Theme	Select Quote(s)
Parenting with Music	"Despite many years of babysitting and being a nanny and then fifteen years of K–12 teaching, nothing has been more informative and inspiring to my teaching than being a parent. There is something unique about being with a child for *so* many hours but also throughout all of the parts of their day. Observing them play, building a relationship, negotiating their needs and their need to be independent. Seeing how they develop in specific nuanced ways. Their more intimate moments are so revealing. The dialog they create between their toys when they think no one is paying attention, the ways they work out their emotions and struggle with relationships and trying new things. This has been so informative. Learning how to support him through the most difficult moments is so challenging. You want to fix it but you have to be supportive while allowing them to work it out."
	"Also, as a parent I've had to set aside all of the impulses to 'teach' in the sort of old-school, traditional, top-down approach to allow him to figure things out for himself. For a long time, I've been inspired by Evelyn Glennie's story of how she was introduced to the snare drum as a young percussionist. She was given the instrument, no sticks, and told to go away and find out all the ways she could 'play' with it and make sounds. It was exploration and discovery based." (Abigail)
	On the Woodlands Orchestra with his daughter: Drumming on trees with sticks, keeping a steady beat, improvising, beatboxing, playing off of each other, recording sounds in nature together, "we were kind of listening to each other and having a little moment, bringing drumsticks to the frozen lake to play." (Gene)
	On her experience with four-and-a-half-year-old son: "That experience in particular has really reminded me about everything that I love about early childhood music education. . . . And it also reminds me how important that this is, observing and experiencing. . . . Music with children at this age is so important to music teacher education. These preservice teachers just really need time with young children. I know they don't get it." (Abigail)

(continued)

Theme	Select Quote(s)
Parenting with Music	"Becoming a parent helped me to be a better teacher. I'm certainly not saying it's that way for everyone. There are good and bad teachers and parents on both sides of the spectrum, but I think for me it's being a parent and learning about kids through my kids. What made it even more interesting and one area I've kind of veered off to lately is both of my kids have learning disabilities; one is autistic and one has dyslexia and ADHD. Working with them, raising them, loving on them, really has helped me to better understand what these what kids who fit their neuro a-typical profile might be experiencing in the classroom." (Shane)
	Bennett talked about learning about teaching through interacting with his own children. He was surprised to observe what musical repertoire and activities his own kids loved from their music classes at school.
Preparation	Bennett pointed to "no preparation for caring and understanding the individual child or development; too much focus on becoming a band director, not enough on understanding children."
	"A course that I really thought was great was childhood development, going over early childhood development through adolescence. For me, I felt that was really important because it's easy as an educator to say, 'Kids will be kids' or 'That's just how they are when they get to middle school' or 'That's just how they are as little kids.' But understanding the reasoning behind that, whether it's physiological or developmental; having an understanding of why kids behave the way that they do." (Trevor)
	"I wish I learned a little bit more about the type of language you use to interact with children of various ages. So far in my student teaching I am thinking about how to speak at the appropriate developmental level." (Nate)
	Bob spoke of the usefulness of courses in psychology and development to better understand children.
	Jack shared that what he learned most about teaching music came directly from working with students. He noted the value of preparation and being able to adapt quickly. His professors taught him that it's okay not to know all the answers, but to be honest and help seek out what you don't know.

Theme	Select Quote(s)
Preparation	"I have a curriculum that I've invented. I'm not saying that I wish my graduate school gave them to me because I'm glad that I sort of found my own identity with what I teach. I found it interesting how much the teacher preparation program lacked." (Kendall)
	Gene on his nontraditional training outside the US: "I didn't do a music degree at first. I did my music education for my master's degree. My initial degree, my undergraduate degree, was in music."
	"I didn't do a music teacher program; my undergrad and my master's was in jazz and classical performance. The first music ed class I ever took was during my doctorate two years ago. So, I learned to teach by teaching. . . . I actually like the fact that I'm coming into teaching and I'm coming into research now. I have a good idea of what a music teacher is because my mom was a thirty-five-year band director." (Shane)
Seeking Options	"Before school, I was focused on one version of what it meant to be a music teacher at the expense of understanding how students and humans interact and that sort of thing."
	On what music could look like/other options to be musical: "It's only in the last couple of years that I've started to realize, I think that actually I don't know if traditional ensembles really did work for me, especially band. When I was young, I liked music and that was the only way to be musical and so I was in band and jazz band and choir and chamber singers in high school and I was in choir and band and middle school. I liked doing it, I liked the social aspect for sure, but that was the only way to be musical. This is before music technology labs really existed. When I was in school, if there was a rock band, I would have loved to have done that. I realized in retrospect, that it just wasn't that option, so I participated in the school musical activities. Those were the only options to be musical." (Bennett)
	Cassidy spoke of her own training in the Kodaly method and folk song repertoire: "I think sometimes there's a lot of windows in folk music, which I loved. I have a Kodaly background, so I feel like I have a little bit of capital and saying this because I do know the folk songs very, very well. But we also want to make sure that we have mirrors in the songs. If we're just singing about wagon wheels and pop pop patches and stuff that's not necessarily in the students' schema. So how do we balance? That was something I really started to pay attention to and pick careful repertoire and careful texts for the students. Seeing the responses

(continued)

Theme	Select Quote(s)
Seeking Options	and the ways that they would talk about what they were learning and how they saw themselves in it; that was an unbelievable discovery that I learned on the job as someone who now prepares future teachers with elementary music methods curriculum." (Cassidy)
Professional Development	Jordan talked about ongoing training in social emotional health through her current job and how she incorporates it into her classroom music activities.
	"I'm an affiliate of Little Kids Rock. I implement all of their curriculum into my classroom. I utilize all the instruments that they donated to me; those are what my students use to perform. I wouldn't be able to teach without Little Kids Rock." (Morgan)
Classroom Insights	"Putting the learning in their [students'] hands and giving them the opportunity to go through the repetitions and figure it out themselves with my guidance, of course, with my facilitation, is really one of the greatest things that I learned in teacher preparation." (Kayla)
	Melody spoke of the value of learning how to create detailed lesson plans.
	"The whole philosophy is student centered and democratic classroom environments. It's a lot easier said than done, of course. Having a student-centered classroom and student-run classroom, having students create norms, having students dictate where your curriculum goes and how you get there, it's a scary thing. It's a scary cliff to jump off of but that's been the most invaluable lesson I've ever learned. I have my students run my entire classroom, essentially, from start to finish. I find a lot more gets done, the more autonomy the students have. At the start of the year, they make their own rules." (Morgan)
	Robert learned to never underestimate children and be careful to witness their natural musical instincts.
	Abigail's graduate work helped her and was "critical and actually it was that kind of thinking that helped pull me out of some of my burnout and made me remember why I love teaching music again."
	Abigail also spoke about her undergraduate studies preparing her with a toolbox of methods she could apply: general music skills, Kodaly, Suzuki, Orff, Dalcroze, and so on.

Theme	Select Quote(s)
Family Mentors	Bennett's father was a band director.
	Shane's mother was a music teacher.
	Kendall talks about a musical family where both parents performed professionally.
	Morgan talked about being an outcast as a child and finding escape and acceptance in music. She talked about strict Arab parents not wanting her to pursue being a music teacher but finding inspiration from a musician uncle.
	Geoffrey refers to strong support from his mother.
Music Teacher Mentors	Bob was inspired by Jack, his high school band director (also our participant), who trusted him to come help teach the marching band after his high school graduation. Now they are colleagues. Bob also refers to a professor in undergrad who inspired him.
	Cassidy was inspired by her upbringing at a constructivist elementary school where her music teacher created a sense of joy and wonder.
	Gene's "amazing mentor" music teacher shared the value of improvisation and creativity. Gene captures a sense of wonder and innocence in music through teaching children. He was drawn to teachers who allowed him to have autonomy and showed him trust and respect.
	Geoffrey's teacher instilled a love of piano, confidence, and ability to explore and question. He was a "mentor who made us believe in ourselves and in the collective group."
	Jack talked about music teachers who showed support and a safe environment for exploration and learning. A college professor was a mentor to talk with. "I always felt supported in my music classes, I was the most confident there, I was the most outgoing and assertive there and I always felt welcomed and included."
	Melody's piano teacher: "Through my early years, the piano was my identity, what I did in my free time, and what brought me peace and joy in a world of mostly chaos. My first music teacher was my piano teacher, Beverley. She gave me a chance when no other teacher wanted me in

(continued)

Theme	Select Quote(s)
Music Teacher Mentors	their studio because I was 'too young.' I always had great respect for her, and now in her memory, years later, I often think that I owe a lot of where my life has taken me to the opportunity she provided me at four years old. She made my childhood dream come true, and it has transformed into a career, but mostly, my way of life."
	Maya's music teacher arranged popular tunes to perform and she found it meaningful.
	Marisol's music teacher inspired confidence in her.
	Robert told us about finding acceptance as a gay child in the South: "I had a lot of wonderful arts teachers, both in music and theater that inspired me to be okay with sharing an aspect of myself, even if I wasn't ready to share all of myself with everyone in a public way. I was embraced and given the right material that was age-appropriate and that really helped me."
	"I remember my music teacher making me feel confident and giving me good advice and being a good friend. I think that music was a time where more students, including myself, could feel a sense of being at home, feeling a place within a larger community, which I believe is probably one of the reasons that so many people gravitate towards music." (Walter)
A Call to Teach Music	"Being a music teacher is such a part of who I am that I can't imagine life without it. I can't imagine not being what I am. This is what I was destined to be: a music teacher." (Jack)
	"My purpose is to teach, to make sure that these kids know that there's at least one space where they know that they're loved. Music is something that should bring joy to them and not bring discomfort or fear." (Kendall)

Works Cited

Alighieri, Dante. 2017. *The Divine Comedy*. n.p.: Aegitas.
Arendt, Hannah. 1961. *Between Past and Future: Six Exercises in Political Thought*. New York: Penguin Books.
———. 2003. *Responsibility and Judgment*. Edited with an introduction by Jerome Kohn. New York: Shoken Books.
Atkins, Dale, and Amanda Salzhauer. 2018. *The Kindness Advantage: Cultivating Compassionate and Connected Children*. New York: Simon and Schuster.
Bassuk, Ellen L., Carmela J. DeCandia, Corey Anne Beach, and Fred Berman. 2014. "America's Youngest Outcasts: A Report Card on Child Homelessness." The National Center on Family Homelessness, American Institutes for Research.
Baudelaire, Charles. 2018. "The Painter of Modern Life." In *Modern Art and Modernism: A Critical Anthology*, edited by Francis Frascina, Charles Harrison, and Deirdre Paul, 23–28. Lanham, MD: Routledge.
Bernstein, Leonard. 1976. *The Unanswered Question: Six Talks at Harvard*. Vol. 33. Cambridge, MA: Harvard University Press.
Beyoncé, et al. 2011, September 12. "Love on Top." Columbia Records.
Brazelton, T. Berry, and Stanley I. Greenspan. 2000. "Our Window to the Future." *Newsweek* 136, no. 17a: 34–36.
———. 2009. *The Irreducible Needs of Children: What Every Child Must Have to Grow, Learn, and Flourish*. Boston: Da Capo Lifelong Books.
Bregman, Rutger. 2019. *Humankind: A Hopeful History*. Translated by Elizabeth Manton and Erica Moore. New York: Little, Brown.
Bruegel, Pieter. n.d. *The Fall of the Rebel Angels*. Brussels, Belgium: Royal Museum of Fine Arts in Belgium.

Caldwell, Sarah, and Harry S. Broudy. 1968. "The Case for Aesthetic Education." *Documentary Report of the Tanglewood Symposium*. Washington, DC: Music Educators National Conference.

Carey, Mariah, and Walter Afanasieff. 1993, October 18. *Hero*. Columbia Records.

Carson, Rachel. 1956/1998. *The Sense of Wonder*. Berkeley, CA: The Nature Company.

Cayari, Christopher, and Heather L. Fox. 2013. "The Pedagogical Implications of the Collaborative Video Log." *2013 Annual Proceedings: On the Practice of Educational Communications and Technology*, 351–63.

Challener, Daniel. 1997. *Stories of Resilience in Childhood: The Narratives of Maya Angelou, Maxine Hong Kingston, Richard Rodriguez, John Edgar Wideman, and Tobias Wolff*. New York: Garland.

Choate, Robert A., ed. 1968. *Documentary Report of the Tanglewood Symposium*. Washington, DC: Music Educators National Conference.

Christakis, Nicholas. 2019. *Blueprint: The Evolutionary Origins of a Good Society*. New York: Little, Brown Spark.

Cleghorn, Sarah N., and Michael Schuman. 2017, January 12. "History of Child Labor in the United States—Part 1: Little Children Working: Monthly Labor Review: U.S. Bureau of Labor Statistics." U.S. Bureau of Labor Statistics. www.bls.gov/opub/mlr/2017/article/history-of-child-labor-in-the-united-states-part-1.htm.

Cohen, Alan. 2002. *Wisdom of the Heart: Inspiration for a Life Worth Living*. Hay Carlsbad, CA: House Lifestyles.

Coles, Robert. 1967. *Children of Crisis: A Study of Courage and Fear*. New York: Little, Brown.

———. 1990. *The Spiritual Life of Children*. New York: Houghton Mifflin Harcourt.

Couenhoven, Jesse. 2005. "St. Augustine's Doctrine of Original Sin." *Augustinian Studies* 36, no. 2: 359–96.

Cunningham, Jennifer. 2005. "Children's Humor." In *Children's Play*, 93–109. Newbury Park, CA: SAGE.

"Daisy Anabelle." n.d. Spotify, open.spotify.com/artist/1HrlMq6MXnQcMeuEuBDnRP. Accessed August 13, 2022.

Dalai Lama. 2022, September 12. "We must educate our young children in the practice of compassion. . . ." Tweet. https://twitter.com/DalaiLama/status/1569257103512211458.

Dalton, Thomas A., and Robert E. Krout. 2005. "Development of the Grief Process Scale Through Music Therapy Songwriting with Bereaved Adolescents." *The Arts in Psychotherapy* 32, no. 2: 131–43.

Dansereau, Diana R. 2020. "Musical Engagement with Young Children Experiencing Homelessness: An Exploratory Study." *Bulletin of the Council for Research in Music Education* 225, 22–44.

Darwin, Charles. 1859. *On the Origin of Species by Means of Natural Selection, or the Preservation of Favoured Races in the Struggle for Life*. London: John Murray.

———. 1871. *The Descent of Man*. London: John Murray.

Davidson, Lyle, Patricia McKernon, and Howard Gardner. 1981. "The Acquisition of Song: A Developmental Approach." *Documentary Report of the Ann Arbor Symposium: Applications of Psychology to the Teaching and Learning of Music.* Reston, VA: Music Educators National Conference.

Dawson, Ben. 2021. "The State of America's Children 2021—Factsheets." Children's Defense Fund. www.childrensdefense.org/state-of-americas-children/soac-2021-factsheets/?gclid=CjwKCAjw9NeXBhAMEiwAbaY4lsmXQBY1yHRDRdnZdjkBZiud.MWHUXSpf1uu4tKtMebzkcOR8CaOkoxoCFBAQAvD_BwE.

Dello Joio, Norman, Abraham H. Maslow, and F. S. C. Northrop. 1981. "The Theoretic and Aesthetic Components in the Western World." *Documentary Report of the Ann Arbor Symposium: Applications of Psychology to the Teaching and Learning of Music.* Reston, VA: Music Educators National Conference.

Dissanayake, Ellen. 2000. *Art and Intimacy: How the Arts Began.* Seattle: University of Washington Press.

Dowling, W. J. 1981. "Mental Structures Through Which Music Is Perceived." *Documentary Report of the Ann Arbor Symposium: Applications of Psychology to the Teaching and Learning of Music.* Reston, VA: Music Educators National Conference.

Editors of Rethinking Schools. 2022, July 21. "Recommitting to the Joyful Classroom." Rethinking Schools. https://rethinkingschools.org/articles/recommitting-to-the-joyful-classroom.

Eisner, Elliot W. 1990. "The Role of Art and Play." In *Children's Play and Learning—Perspectives and Policy Implications,* edited by Edgar Klugman and Sara Smilansky, 43–56. New York: Columbia University, Teachers College Press.

Ekman, Paul. 1993. "Facial Expression and Emotion." *American Psychologist* 48, no. 4: 384.

Elliot, Andrea. 2013, December 8. "Invisible Child: Dasani's Homeless Life." *New York Times.* www.nytimes.com/projects/2013/invisible-child/index.html#/?chapt=1.

———. 2021. *Invisible Child: Poverty, Survival and Hope in an American City.* New York: Random House.

Emerson, Ralph Waldo. 2003. *Nature and Selected Essays.* New York: Penguin.

Fairchild, Rebecca, and Katrina Skewes McFerran. 2019. "Music Is Everything: Using Collaborative Group Songwriting as an Arts-Based Method with Children Experiencing Homelessness and Family Violence." *Nordic Journal of Music Therapy* 28, no. 2: 88–107.

Ferguson, Brian, R. 2018, September 1. "War Is Not Part of Human Nature." *Scientific American.* www.scientificamerican.com/article/war-is-not-part-of-human-nature/?redirect=1, 10.1038/scientificamerican0918-76.

Fineberg, Jonathan. 1997. *The Innocent Eye: Children's Art and the Modern Artist.* Princeton, NJ: Princeton University Press.

Fiore, Jennifer. 2016. "Analysis of Lyrics from Group Songwriting with Bereaved Children and Adolescents." *Journal of Music Therapy* 53, no. 3: 207–31.

Fox, Heather L., and Christopher Cayari. 2016. "Graduate Students' Readiness and Perceptions of the Pedagogical Application of Collaborative Video Logs." *TechTrends* 60, no. 6: 585–90.

Freire, Paulo. 1992. *Pedagogy of Hope: Reliving Pedagogy of the Oppressed*. New York: Continuum.

Freud, Sigmund. 1955. "Beyond the Pleasure Principle." In *The Standard Edition of the Complete Psychological Works of Sigmund Freud, Volume XVIII (1920–1922): Beyond the Pleasure Principle, Group Psychology and Other Works*, 1–64.

Frost, Joe L., Sue Clark Wortham, and Robert Stuart Reifel. 2008. *Play and Child Development*. Upper Saddle River, NJ: Pearson/Merrill Prentice Hall.

Gellel, Adrian-Mario. 2013. "Children and Spirituality." In *The Routledge International Handbook of Spirituality in Society and the Professions*, edited by László Zsolnai and Bernadette Flanagan, 120–26. London: Routledge.

Ginott, Haim G. 1972. *Teacher and Child: A Book for Parents and Teachers*. New York: Macmillan.

Griffiths, Education Fleur. 2013. "The Talking Table: Sharing Wonder in Early Childhood Education." In *Wonder-Full Education*, edited by Kieran Egan, Annabella Cant, and Gillian Judson, 130–42. New York: Routledge.

Grudin, R. 1990. *The Grace of Great Things: Creativity and Innovation*. New York: Ticknor & Fields.

Hamilton, Laura S., Brian M. Stecher, and Kun Yuan. 2012. "Standards-Based Accountability in the United States: Lessons Learned and Future Directions." *Education Inquiry* 3, no. 2: 149–70.

Hansen, D. T. 1995. *The Call to Teach*. New York: Teachers College Press.

———. 2021. *Reimagining the Call to Teach: A Witness to Teachers and Teaching*. New York: Teachers College Press.

Hare, Brian. 2017."Survival of the Friendliest: Homo Sapiens Evolved via Selection for Prosociality." *Annual Review of Psychology* 68, 155–86.

Hare, Brian, and Vanessa Woods. 2020. *Survival of the Friendliest: Understanding Our Origins and Rediscovering Our Common Humanity*. New York: Random House.

Harris, Maria. 1991. *Teaching and Religious Imagination: An Essay in the Theology of Teaching*. San Francisco, CA: HarperCollins.

Hay, David, and Rebecca Nye. 1998/2006. *The Spirit of the Child*. London: HarperCollins.

Hendricks, Karin S. 2018. *Compassionate Music Teaching: A Framework for Motivation and Engagement in the 21st Century*. Lanham, MD: Rowman & Littlefield.

Hobbes, Thomas. 1651. *Leviathan*.

Huebner, Dwayne E. 1999. *The Lure of the Transcendent: Collected Essays by Dwayne E. Huebner*. Edited by Vikki Hillis. Collected and introduced by William F. Pinar. Mahwah, NJ: Lawrence Erlbaum.

Huizinga, Johan. 1938/1950. *Homo Ludens: A Study of the Play-Element in Culture*. Boston: Beacon.

Hume, David. 1896. *A Treatise of Human Nature*. Clarendon Press.

Izzard, Eddie. 2010, March 30. "Eddie Izzard 'World History' Sketch from Dress to Kill." YouTube. www.youtube.com/watch?v=hxQYE3E8dEY.
Johnson, Steven. 2010. *Where Good Ideas Come From: The Natural History of Innovation*. New York: Riverhead.
Keltner, Dacher. 2009. *Born to Be Good: The Science of a Meaningful Life*. New York: W. W. Norton.
Kessen, William. 1981. "Encounters: The American Child's Meeting with Music." *Documentary Report of the Ann Arbor Symposium: Applications of Psychology to the Teaching and Learning of Music*. Reston, VA: Music Educators National Conference.
Keys, Alicia, et al. 2012, September 4. "Girl on Fire." RCA Records.
Knight, Susan Dyer. 2010. "A Study of Adult Non-singers in Newfoundland." PhD diss., Institute of Education, University of London.
Kratus, John. 2016. "Songwriting: A New Direction for Secondary Music Education." *Music Educators Journal* 102, no. 3: 60–65.
Krueger, Joel. 2013. "Empathy, Enaction, and Shared Musical Experience: Evidence from Infant Cognition." In *The Emotional Power of Music: Multidisciplinary Perspectives on Musical Arousal, Expression, and Social Control*, edited by Tom Cochrane, Bernardino Fantini, and Klaus R. Scherer. Oxford: Oxford University Press. https://doi.org/10.1093/acprof:oso/9780199654888.003.0014.
Leinsdorf, Erich. 1968. "Music in a Changing World." *Documentary Report of the Tanglewood Symposium*. Washington, DC: Music Educators National Conference.
Levitin, Daniel J. 2006. *This Is Your Brain on Music: The Science of a Human Obsession*. New York: Penguin.
"Little Kids Rock | Music Education Nonprofit." n.d. Little Kids Rock, www.littlekidsrock.org.
Littleton, Danette. 1991. "Influence of Play Settings on Preschool Children's Music and Play Behaviors." PhD diss. University of Texas at Austin.
———. 2015. *When Music Goes to School: Perspectives on Learning and Teaching*. Lanham, MD: Rowman & Littlefield.
———. 2016. *Toward a Pedagogy of Compassion*. Presentation at the University of Cambridge, United Kingdom, Building Interdisciplinary Bridges Across Cultures Conference.
———. 2022. "Song Lines and Soundtracks: Autoethnographic Narratives Across Four Generations." *Journal of Popular Music Education* 6, no. 1: 101–16.
Lloyd Webber, Julian. 1985. *Song of the Birds: Sayings, Stories, and Impressions of Pablo Casals*. London: Robson Books.
Locke, John. 1847. *An Essay Concerning Human Understanding*. Philadelphia, PA: Kay & Troutman.
Madsen, Clifford, ed. 2020. *Vision 2020: The Housewright Symposium on the Future of Music Education*. Lanham, MD: Rowman & Littlefield.
Manuel-Miranda, Lin. 2015. "Aaron Burr, Sir." *Hamilton: An American Musical (Original Broadway Cast Recording)*. Performances by Lin-Manuel Miranda, Leslie Odom Jr., Phillipa Soo, and Jonathan Groff. Atlantic Records.

Mark, Michael L. 2020. "MENC: From Tanglewood to the Present." In *Vision 2020: The Housewright Symposium on Music Education*, 5–22. Lanham, MD: Rowman & Littlefield.

Marshall, Samuel Lyman Atwood. 1947/2000. *Men Against Fire: The Problem of Battle Command*. Norman: University of Oklahoma Press.

Mayberry, Lindsay Satterwhite, Marybeth Shinn, Jessica Gibbons Benton, and Jasmine Wise. 2014. "Families Experiencing Housing Instability: The Effects of Housing Programs on Family Routines and Rituals." *American Journal of Orthopsychiatry* 84, no. 1: 95.

Mead, Margaret. 1951. *Research in Contemporary Cultures*. Pittsburgh, PA: Carnegie Mellon University Press.

Mendelowitz, Daniel Marcus. 1953. *Children Are Artists: An Introduction to Children's Art for Teachers and Parents*. Redwood City, CA: Stanford University Press.

———. 2016. *Thriving*. New York: Macmillan.

Miller, Arthur. 1971. *The Crucible*. Harmondsworth, UK: Viking.

Miller, Lisa. 2013. *The Spiritual Child: The New Science on Parenting for Health and Lifelong Thriving*. New York: St. Martin's Press.

Miró, Joan, and Jacques Dupin. 1993. *Miró*. Spain: Polígrafa.

Montagu, Ashley. 1989. *Growing Young*. Westport, CT: Greenwood.

Nathan, Robert. 1935. "The Heart in Wonder, Like a Lonely Wren." In *Selected Poems of Robert Nathan*, "Sonnet VI." New York: Alfred A Knopf.

Noddings, Nel. 2005a. *The Challenge to Care in Schools: An Alternative Approach to Education*. New York: Teachers College Press.

———. 2005b. "Identifying and Responding to Needs in Education." *Cambridge Journal of Education* 35, no. 2: 147–59.

Northern Plains Reservation Aid. 2011. "Native American History and Culture: Boarding Schools—American Indian Relief Council Is Now Northern Plains Reservation Aid." www.nativepartnership.org/site/PageServer?pagename=airc_hist_boardingschools.

Nortjé, Elsabe, and Liesl Van der Merwe. 2016. "Young Children and Spirituality: Understanding Children's Connectedness in a Group Music Class." *International Journal of Children's Spirituality* 21, no. 1: 3–18.

Ong, Wei Ann, Suyansah Swanto, and Asmaa Alsaqqaf. 2020. "Engaging in Reflective Practice via Vlogs: Experience of Malaysian ESL Pre-Service Teachers." *Indonesian Journal of Applied Linguistics* 9: 716–24.

Orff, Carl. 1937, June 8. *Carmina Burana: Cantiones Profanae Cantoribus et Choris Cantandae Comitantibus Instrumentis Atque Imaginibus Magicis*. Alte Oper, Frankfort am Main, Germany: Premier Performance.

Paley, Vivian Gussin. 1991. *The Boy Who Would Be a Helicopter: The Uses of Storytelling in the Classroom*. Cambridge, MA: Harvard University Press.

———. 1993. *You Can't Say You Can't Play*. Cambridge, MA: Harvard University Press.

———. 1999. *The Kindness of Children*. Cambridge, MA: Harvard University Press.

Palmer, P. J. 2017. *The Courage to Teach: Exploring the Inner Landscape of a Teacher's Life*. San Francisco, CA: Jossey-Bass.

Parten, Mildred B. 1932. "Social Participation Among Pre-School Children." *The Journal of Abnormal and Social Psychology* 27, no. 3: 243.

Pasiali, Varvara. 2012. "Resilience, Music Therapy, and Human Adaptation: Nurturing Young Children and Families." *Nordic Journal of Music Therapy* 21, no. 1: 36–56.

Piaget, Jean. 1962. *Play, Dreams and Imitation in Childhood*. Translated by C. Gattegno and F. M. Hodgson. New York: W. W. Norton.

Polanyi, Michael. 1958. *Personal Knowledge Toward a Post-Critical Philosophy*. Chicago, IL: University of Chicago Press.

———. 1966/2009. *The Tacit Dimension*. Garden City, NY: Doubleday.

Randles, Clint. 2018. "Modern Band: A Descriptive Study of Teacher Perceptions." *Journal of Popular Music Education* 2, no. 3: 217–30.

Reimer, Bennett. 2009. *Seeking the Significance of Music Education: Essays and Reflections*. Lanham, MD: Rowman & Littlefield Education.

Roberts, Melina. 2006. "'I Want to Play and Sing My Story': Home-Based Songwriting for Bereaved Children and Adolescents." *Australian Journal of Music Therapy* 17: 18–34.

Root-Bernstein, Michèle. 2014. *Inventing Imaginary Worlds: From Childhood Play to Adult Creativity Across the Arts and Sciences*. Lanham, MD: Rowman & Littlefield.

Rousseau, Jean-Jacques. 1899. *Émile, or Treatise on Education*. Vol. 20. Appleton.

Sample, Katherine. 2019. "The Soundtrack of Homelessness: A Study of Music Use Among Homeless Youth and Recommendations for Music Therapists Who Serve Them." PhD diss. Arizona State University.

Schei, Tiri Bergesen, and Edvin Schei. 2017. "Voice Shame: Self-Censorship in Vocal Performance." *The Singing Network* 1.

Schuller, Gunther, and Ralph W. Tyler. 1968. "The Role of Music in Our Philosophy of Education." *Documentary Report of the Tanglewood Symposium*. Washington, DC: Music Educators National Conference.

Schuman, Michael. 2017, January. "History of Child Labor in the United States—Part 1: Little Children Working," *Monthly Labor Review*, U.S. Bureau of Labor Statistics. https://doi.org/10.21916/mlr.2017.1.

Shakur, Tupac. 2000, November 21. "The Rose That Grew from Concrete." Amaru/Interscope Records.

Smilansky, Sara. 1968. *The Effects of Sociodramatic Play on Disadvantaged Preschool Children*. Hoboken, NJ: Wiley.

Sole, Meryl, and Claudia Calì, eds. 2022. "Special Issue on Popular Music in the Family Context." *Journal of Popular Music Education* 6, no. 1: 5–23.

Solomon, Maynard. 1995. *Mozart: A Life*. New York: HarperCollins.

Star Wars. 1977. George Lucas, Lucasfilms Ltd.

Staum, Myra J. 1993. "A Music/Non-music Intervention with Homeless Children." *Journal of Music Therapy* 30, no. 4: 236–62.

Thomas, Paul Lee, ed. 2015. *Pedagogies of Kindness and Respect: On the Lives and Education of Children*. New York: Peter Lang.
Trehub, Sandra E. 2003. "Musical Predispositions in Infancy: An Update." In *The Cognitive Neuroscience of Music*, edited by I. Peretz and R. Zatorre, 3–20. Oxford: Oxford University Press. https://doi.org/10.1093/acprof:oso/9780198525202.003.0001.
Tutu, Desmond, and Mpho Tutu. 2010. *Made for Goodness: And Why This Makes All the Difference*. New York: HarperCollins.
U.S. Congress. 2001. Public Law, PL 107-110, *No Child Left Behind Act*.
U.S. Congress. 2015. Public Law, S.1177, *Every Student Succeeds Act*.
U.S. National Commission on Excellence in Education. 1983. *A Nation at Risk: The Imperative for Educational Reform*.
Van der Merwe, Liesl, and John Habron. 2015. "A Conceptual Model of Spirituality in Music Education." *Journal of Research in Music Education* 63, no. 1: 47–69.
Vandross, Luther. 1981. "A House Is Not a Home." Epic Records. Burt Bacharach and Hal David.
Van Manen, Max. 1990. *Researching Lived Experience: Human Science for an Action Sensitive Pedagogy*. Albany: State University of New York Press.
———. 2016. *The Tact of Teaching: The Meaning of Pedagogical Thoughtfulness*. Abingdon, Oxon: Routledge.
Villalpando, Nicole. 2021, October 11. "The Kindness Campaign Wants to Teach the World to Write a Song Through New Kind Music." *Austin American-Statesman*. www.austin360.com/story/lifestyle/family/2021/10/11/kindness-campaign-teaches-songwriting-social-emotional-learning-through-new-kind-music/6008018001.
Welch, Graham F. 2012. *The Benefits of Singing for Children*. London: Institute for Education, University of London.
Wennerstrand, Anne L. 2021. "The Playful Ways of the Performing Artist." In *Play from Birth to Twelve and Beyond*, edited by Doris Pronin Fromberg and Doris Bergen, 442–48. London: Routledge.
Whitehead, Alfred North. 1929/1963. *Aims of Education*. New York: Macmillan.
Wills, Ruth. 2011. "The Magic of Music: A Study into the Promotion of Children's Well-Being Through Singing." *International Journal of Children's Spirituality* 16, no. 1: 37–46.
Wilson, Ruth A. 2010. "Aesthetics and a Sense of Wonder." *Exchange*.
Wordsworth, William. 1802. "My Heart Leaps Up." In *The Norton Anthology of English Literature* 2, 335.
"Workshops and Residencies." n.d. Beth and Scott and Friends. Accessed August 13, 2022. bethandscott.net/schoolworkshopsandresidencies.
Zillmann, Dolf, and Su-lin Gan. 1997. "Musical Taste in Adolescence." In *The Social Psychology of Music*, edited by D. J. Hargreaves and A. C. North, 161–87. Oxford: Oxford University Press.
Zimmerman, Marilyn P. 1981. "Child Development and Music Education." *Documentary Report of the Ann Arbor Symposium*. Reston, VA: Music Educators National Conference.

Index

Abigail (participant), 23, 54; study data from, 94–95, 97, 102–3, 107, 110
acceptance, 24; kindness as, 16–17; mentorship and, 69, 111–12. *See also* belonging
ADHD. *See* Attention-deficit/hyperactivity disorder
adolescence, 19–20; spirituality in, 41–43
affective neuroscience, 10
The Aims of Education (Whitehead), 77–78
Alice (participant), 7, 10, 24, 27, 33, 80; study data from, 90–91, 93–94, 105
analysis: data, xii; of music, 41–42
Andy (participant), study data from, 104–5
anonymity, in studies, xviin1
anthropology: cultural, xi; social, xiv
Arendt, Hannah, 82–83
Ari (music student), 41–43
art: education as, 70; performance and, 56–57; worldplay influencing, 61–62
Art and Intimacy (Dissanayake), 16

artists, childhood memories and, 61–62
"The Art of Teaching" (Huebner), 70–71
Atkins, Dale, 16–17
Attention-deficit/hyperactivity disorder (ADHD), 27
Augustin of Hippo, 4

behavior, 8–9, 11, 30, 93; ethical, 85
belief, xiii–xiv, 3–4, 6; in music educators, 83
belonging, 24, 95–97
The Benefits of Singing for Children (Welch), 14–15
Bennett (participant), 24–25, 68, 81; study data from, 97, 104, 106, 108–9, 111
Bierko, Beth, 19–20
Bierko, Scott, 19–20
Bob (participant), 68, 81; study data from, 94–95, 108
Born to Be Good (Keltner), 5
The Boy Who Would Be a Helicopter (Paley), 6
Brazelton, T. Berry, xv, 23

Bregman, Rutger, 5
Brooklyn, New York, 29
Bureau of Indian Affairs, ix

care, 21; challenge of, 17; ethics of, 12–13, 17, 85; foster, 30–31; music educators and, 16; in relationships, 90–91, 94
Carey, Mariah, 11
Carson, Rachel, 59–60
Casals, Pablo, 15–16
Cassidy (participant), 33, 63, 69; study data from, 89–91, 104–5, 109–11
The Challenge of Care in Schools (Noddings), 17
challenges, 94–95; of care, 17; facing music educators, 80–81; of meeting needs, 26
children. *See* students
"Children and Spirituality" (Gellel), 41
Children of Crisis (Coles), 34
classroom, music: as hostile environment, 13, 15–16; insights from, 110; lessons compared to plans in, 26–27
Coles, Robert: *Children of Crisis*, 34; *Spiritual Lives of Children*, 34–35
communication: in play, 52; voice and, 15
compassion, 85; music education and, 12–13, 21; pedagogy of, 87
Compassionate Music Teaching (Hendricks), 12–13
connectedness: music education and, 36–37; between self and other, 17
constructive play, 50
controversy, of kindness, 86
The Courage to Teach (Palmer), 67–68
COVID-19 pandemic, x
creativity, 54, 69, 102
cultural anthropology, xi
cycle, of learning, 77–78

Daisy (participant), 20
Dansereau, Diana, 32
Darwin, Charles, xiv; *Descent*, 86; emotions studied by, 9–10; goodness and, 5
Dasani (music student), 29–31, 32n2, 69–70
data, 89–112; analysis of, xii
Descent (Darwin), 86
development, 90; play and, 56–58; professional, 110
developmental differences, 102
disruptive students, 8–9; empathy and, 17–18
Dissanayake, Ellen, 7–8, 73; *Art and Intimacy*, 16
diversity, 103
dramatic play, 47–49

education, ix–x, 78; as art, 70. *See also* music education
educators, music. *See* music educators
Ekman, Paul, Facial Action Coding System of, 10
Elliot, Andrea, 28–32, 32n2
embarrassment, of students, 13, 16
emotions, 100; studied by Darwin, 9–10
empathy, 12, 85; disruptive students and, 17–18; experience of music and, 35; in music education, xi
Empathy, Enaction, and Shared Musical Experience (Krueger), 35
Engagement with Young Children Experiencing Homelessness (Dansereau), 32
the Enlightenment, 4, 86
ethics of care, 12–13, 17
evolution, of music, 15
examples, of musical play, 47–53, 55–56
experience, of music, 36; empathy and, 35
explicit knowing, xv, 34, 36

exploration, in play, 50–51
expression, 25; of individuality, 12; of self, 19

Facial Action Coding System (Ekman), 10
Fair Labor Standards Act, x
family, 111; mentorship and, 68–69; music and, 20, 31, 71–73
feelings, 13–14, 37, 63, 86–87
Ferguson, R. Brian, xiv
flow, music students and, 37–38
foster care, 30–31
freedom, wonder and, 64
functional play, 50–51

Gabriela (participant), 13–14
games, 51, 58n1. *See also* play, musical
Gellel, Adrian-Mario, 41
Gene (participant), 25, 54, 69; study data from, 90, 93–95, 99, 103, 107, 109, 111
Geoffrey (participant), 68, 70; study data from, 90, 106, 111
goodness, xiii–xiv, 89; Darwin and, 5; innate, 3–4, 6–7, 10; music educators and, 73; spirituality and, 39–40
Grace (participant), 70; study data from, 90, 102
Greenspan, Stanley I., xv, 23
group play, 52–53
Growing Young (Montagu), xv

Hay, David, 38–40
heavy metal music, 41–43
Hendricks, Karin, 12–13
"Hero," 11
home, school compared to, 30
homelessness, children and, 28, 32; foster care and, 30–31; mentorship and, 69–70; "parentified" children and, 29

hope, pedagogy and, 82–83
Hopi, 34–35
hostile environment, music classroom as, 13, 15–16
Huebner, Dwayne, 70–71
Humankind (Bregman), 5
human nature, 3, 5; war and, xiv
humor, in play, 55–56

identity, 21; adolescence and, 41–42; spirituality and, 39; voice and, 14, 19
imitation, play and, 50, 52
improvisation: music education and, 54; during play, 49–50
inclusion, of children, 25–26
Indian Child Welfare Act, ix
individuality, 12, 25, 90; music play and, 53; spirituality and, 38–39
inequality, ix–x, 32n2
innate traits, of children, xv, 64, 80; basic needs and, 23; goodness, 3–4, 6–7, 10; musicality as, 53–54, 62
inspiration, music educators and, 63
instinct, against killing, 4–5
Institutional Review Board, xviin1
instruments, playing, 47–49, 52, 72; compared with songwriting, 21
Inventing Imaginary Worlds (Root-Bernstein), 60–63
"Invisible Child" (Elliot), 28–32
The Irreducible Needs of Children (Brazelton and Greenspan), xv, 23

Jack (participant), 17–18, 33, 69–70; study data from, 93, 96, 99–100, 106, 108, 111–12
Joe (participant), study data from, 90, 92
Jordan (participant), 8–9, 10, 25, 33, 80; study data from, 92, 100, 105, 110
Journal for Popular Music Education, 31

joy, 16, 58, 82. *See also* wonder
Julia (participant), 27; study data from, 93, 97, 99, 102

Katie (participant), 69
Kayla (participant), 7–8, 10; study data from, 90–91, 102, 110
Keltner, Dacher, 5
Kendall (participant), 27–28, 68, 81; study data from, 99–100, 109, 111–12
Kendra (participant), 25; study data from, 101
killing, instinct against, 4–5
kindness, xiv–xv, 11, 16–17, 21, 85, 87; controversy of, 86; music educators and, 73; spirituality and, 39–40
The Kindness Advantage (Atkins and Salzhauer), 16–17
Kindness Campaign, 20
The Kindness of Children (Paley), 6
knowing: prelinguistic, 35; tacit and explicit, xv, 34, 36. *See also* understanding
Krista (participant), study data from, 104
Krueger, Joel, 35

Laura (participant), 15
LaVerne (participant), 13
learning: cycle of, 77–78; individualized, 100–101; play and, 57, 74–75; reciprocity and, 85; recommendations for, 40, 79–82; understanding children and, 3–4, 7, 77
Lennon, John, 19
Levitin, Daniel J., 15
Lincoln, Abraham, 5
listening, 42, 57, 88, 97
Little Kids Rock, Modern Band workshops through, 20–21
love: music educators and, 70–71; pedagogy and, 82

Madama Butterfly (Puccini), 36
Marisol (participant), 26; study data from, 96–97, 101, 112
Marshall, Samuel, 4
Maya (participant), 13; study data from, 95, 97, 103, 112
McCartney, Paul, 19
McKinney's School for the Arts, Brooklyn, 29
Melissa (participant), 81
Melody (participant), 18, 68–69; study data from, 94, 103, 110–11
memories, of childhood, 71–73; artists and, 61–62; music educators and, 57–58, 63
Men Against Fire (Marshall), 4
mentorship: family and, 68–69; music educators and, 70, 111–12
methodology, of studies, xi–xii
Milton Hershey School, Pennsylvania, 29–30
mindfulness, 105
modeling, 92
Modern Band workshops, through Little Kids Rock, 20–21
Montagu, Ashley, xv
Morgan (participant), 9–10, 16, 27, 68, 81; study data from, 91–93, 95–96, 98, 100, 103, 110–11
motivations, of music educators, xvi, 67
music, xvi, 36; evolution of, 15; family and, 20, 31, 71–73; heavy metal, 41–43; natural, 53; playing instruments and, 47–49, 52, 72; popular, 11, 31–32; spirituality and, 33; transformation and, 37–39; wonder-filled, 60, 63–64, 104
musical independence, 102
musicality, 103; in children, 53–54, 62; music educators and, 74–75
musical play, 47–52, 54–55, 104–5; listening to, 57; playing music contrasted with, 53, 56

Musical Predispositions in Infancy (Trehub), 35
music education, 32, 62, 70; compassion and, 12–13, 21; connectedness and, 36–37; empathy in, xi; improvisation and, 54
music educators, x, 75, 82–83; care and, 16; challenges facing, 80–81; childhood memories of, 57–58, 63; inspiration and, 63; love and, 70–71; mentorship and, 68–70, 111–12; motivations of, xvi, 67; role reversals and, 41–43; spirituality and, 35–36, 71, 74; training of, xiii; understanding and, 87; values of, 73–74
music students: Ari, 41–43; Dasani, 29–31, 32n2, 69–70; flow and, 37–38; Yolanda, 11–12, 40, 43

Nate (participant), 81; study data from, 93, 98, 108
National Association for Music Education, xvi
natural music making, 53
needs, of children, xiii, 23–24, 74, 93; challenges of meeting, 26; homelessness and, 31; inclusion, 25–26; special, 27–32
neuroscience, affective, 10
Noddings, Nel, 17
Nortje, Elsabe, 36–37
nurturing relationships, 24–25
Nye, Rebecca, 38–40

objectives, of music education, 78
options, seeking, 109–10
other, connection to self of, 17

Padgett, Deborah K., 28, 30
Paley, Vivian, xi, 5, 7, 57; *The Boy Who Would Be a Helicopter*, 6; *The Kindness of Children*, 6; *You Can't Say You Can't Play*, 6

Palmer, Parker, 71; *The Courage to Teach*, 67–68
parallel play, 52
"parentified child," 29
parenting, 99–100; with music, 107–8
Parten, Mildred B., 51–52
participants: themes for, xii, 85–112. *See also specific participants*
participation, in knowing, 35
pedagogy: of compassion, 87; hope and, 82–83; worldplay and, 64
pedagogy, study category of: co-players, 103; creativity, 102; developmental differences, 102; diversity, 103; mindfulness, 105; musical independence, 102; musicality, 103; musical play, 104–5; remarkable moments, 102; responsive teaching, 103; sharing, 103; spiritual experiences, 106; spiritual practices, 105; wonder-filled music, 104
Pennsylvania, 29–30
performance, 8, 37, 42, 82; art and, 56–57; play and, 52
perspective, of a child, xi, 53; music from, 36; spirituality from, 34–35
perspectives, study category of: behavior, 93; belonging, 95–97; care and respect, 91; caring relationships, 90–91, 94; challenges, 94–95; development, 90; emotions, 100; goodness, 89; individuality, 90; individualized learning, 100–101; listening, 97; modeling, 92; needs of children, 93; parenting, 99–100; relationships, 97–99; respect, 99; safety, 101; special needs, 99; surpassing teacher duties, 91; understanding, 93; wonder, 90
play, musical, 53, 55; cognitive, 51; communication in, 52; co-players and, 54, 103; development and, 56–58; dramatic, 47–49; functional,

50–51; improvisation during, 49–50; music education and, 57, 74–75; performance and, 52; seriousness contrasted with, 56–57; sharing during, 48–50; solitary, 51–52; wonder and, 60
playing music: instruments and, 47–49, 52, 72; musical play contrasted with, 53, 56
Polanyi, Michael, xv, 34
popular music, 11, 31–32
Powell, Bryan, 20–21
prelinguistic knowing, 35
preparation, 108–9
pretend, playing, 47–49
professional development, 110
promises, study category of: call to teach music, 112; classroom insights, 110; family members, 111; music teacher mentors, 111–12; parenting with music, 107–8; preparation, 108–9; professional development, 110; seeking options, 109–10
public education reforms, 78
Puccini, Giacomo, 36

reciprocity, music education and, 85
recommendations: musical play and, 54; for music education, 40, 79–82
reforms, in public education, 78
refuge, school as, 29, 31
Reimer, Bennett, 81–82
relationality, 40, 43
relationships, 97–99; caring, 90–91; nurturing, 24–25
remarkable moments, 102
Researching Lived Experience (Van Manen), 37
respect, xi, 10–12, 69, 99
Rhett (participant), study data from, 104
Robert (participant), 26, 69, 81; study data from, 96–97, 100, 103, 110, 112

role reversal, 41–43
Roosevelt, Franklin Delano, x
Root-Bernstein, Michèle, 60–63

safety, 23–24, 69, 101
Salzhauer, Amanda, 16–17
school, 56–57; compared to home, 30; as refuge, 29, 31
Seeking the Significance of Music Education (Reimer), 81–82
self: connected to other, 17; expression of, 19, 25
sense, making, 34
The Sense of Wonder (Carson), 59–60
sensory processing disorder, 28
seriousness, play contrasted with, 56–57
Shakur, Tupac, 32
Shane (participant), 17, 68; study data from, 92, 98, 100, 108–9, 111
sharing, 103; of feelings, 13–14, 37, 63, 86–87; during play, 48–50
singing, 14–15; memories of, 71–72
skills, developing, 42
Smilansky, Sara, cognitive play categories of, 51
social anthropology, xiv
social participation taxonomy, 51–52
sociology, xi
solitary play, 51–52
songwriting, 19–20; compared with playing instruments, 21
special needs, for children, 99; ADHD and, 27; homelessness, 29–32; sensory processing disorder as, 28
Spirit of the Child (Hay and Nye), 38–40
spirituality, 105–6; in adolescence, 41–43; from child's perspective, 34–35; connectedness and, 36–37; goodness and, 39–40; identity and, 39; individuality of, 38–39; kindness and, 39–40; music and, 33; music educators and, 35–36, 71, 74; transformation and, 40, 42

Spiritual Lives of Children (Coles), 34–35
students: disruptive, 8–9, 17–18; embarrassment of, 13, 16; individuality in, 12; joy and, 16, 58, 82; transformation in, 12. *See also* music students
study: anonymity in, xviin1; methodology of, xi–xii; pedagogy category in, 102–6; personal stories in, 67; perspectives category in, 89–101; promises category in, 107–12; video reflections, xii
surpassing teacher duties, 91
symposia, 78–80

The Tacit Dimension (Polanyi), 34
tacit knowing, xv, 34, 36
The Tact of Teaching (Van Manen), 82–83
Tanglewood Declaration, 79–80
Tara (participant), 8, 10; study data from, 98–99, 102
teachers. *See* music educators
teaching: call to, 112; responsive, 103
tenement children, ix
themes, for participants, xii, 85–112
This Is Your Brain on Music (Levitin), 15
Tom (participant), study data from, 95
training, for music educators, xiii
transcendence, students and, 37
transformation, 12; music and, 37–39; spiritual, 40, 42
Trehub, Sandra, 35
Trevor (participant), 8, 10, 70, 81; study data from, 100–101, 108

understanding, 93; mentorship and, 68–69; in music education, 3–4, 7, 77; music educators and, 80, 87; seeking, 63

values, of music educators, 73–74
Van der Merwe, Liesl, 36–37
Van Manen, Max, 40; *Researching Lived Experience*, 37; *The Tact of Teaching*, 82–83
video ethnographies, xii
vignettes, 71–73
virtuosity, 43
voice: communication and, 15; identity and, 14, 19

Walter (participant), 69; study data from, 112
war, human nature and, xiv
"War Is Not a Part of Human Nature" (Ferguson), xiv
Welch, Graham, 14–15
Whitehead, Alfred North, 62; *The Aims of Education*, 77–78
Wills, Ruth, 37–38
wonder, 74, 90; mentorship and, 69; music and, 104; worldplay and, 60–61
workshops, by Bierko, B., and Bierko, S., 19–20
worldplay, 60–63; pedagogy and, 64
World War II, 4–5

Yolanda (music student), 11–12, 40, 43
You Can't Say You Can't Play (Paley), 6
Young Composers Project (symposium), 78–79h

About the Authors

Danette Littleton, PhD, University of Texas–Austin, master's and bachelor's degrees in music education, Florida State University. Musical training in piano, voice, and choral conducting led Dr. Littleton to a career in music as a director of children's choirs, music teacher with students from prekindergarten through secondary school, and professor, researcher, and arts education consultant. Her recent academic and career positions include professor of music and music education, University of Tennessee, and music teacher, Del Prado Elementary School, Boca Raton, Florida. She was appointed director of arts education projects funded by the National Endowment for the Arts, the Getty Foundation, Head Start, Wolf Trap Institute for Early Learning in the Arts, Sesame Street Workshop, Leonard Bernstein Center, Gibson Guitar Corporation, and the Grammy Foundation. As a presenter, she was invited to speak on children's musical development, spontaneous musical play, musicality and spirituality, and pedagogy of care and compassion. These engagements took place at conferences and universities in the United States, Canada, England, Japan, Korea, Sweden, and South Africa. Danette has authored forty publications in books and journals and a professional book, *When Music Goes to School: Perspectives on Learning and Teaching* (2015, Rowman & Littlefield). As an independent scholar, she continues to study, teach, and write about the emergence of human musicality from infancy through childhood, when learning is most fervent and sensitivity to music most vibrant.

Meryl Sole, EdD, is a music educator, researcher, and French horn player. She holds a doctorate in music and music education from Teachers College, Columbia University, including a master's degree in brass performance (Boston University) and a bachelor's degree in music theory (University of Pennsylvania). Currently, she teaches graduate and undergraduate courses in music education at New York University and Teachers College, Columbia University. Dr. Sole held full-time music faculty positions at the University of New Haven, Bergen Community College, and SUNY Empire State College. Dr. Sole is an active researcher focusing on early childhood music, where she explores musical parenting and musical development through toddlers' spontaneous "crib songs." Additionally, she studies creative approaches in music theory pedagogy and popular music in families. Dr. Sole's research has been published in peer-reviewed journals and presented at numerous national and international conferences.

www.ingramcontent.com/pod-product-compliance
Lightning Source LLC
Chambersburg PA
CBHW032028230426
43671CB00005B/234